Dedication

I dedicate this book to Gary Douglas and Dr. Dain Heer.

When I think of Access Consciousness®, I automatically think, "GaryDain." These two men are changing our planet and in a very BIG way! If there is a possibility for it to survive, it will be greatly due to their contribution of consciousness.

I have no words for Gary Douglas. What do you say to someone who has literally given YOU back to you? Here I was looking for the REAL ME my whole life, in every nook and cranny I could find, and then one glorious day I listened to a class he'd facilitated—that was the beginning of everything that I've always known was possible. As I heard his language of consciousness, it pulled aside the insanity of this world, like Toto pulling the Wizard's curtain. Life has not been the same since. More, Better, Greater, please!

Gary's language of consciousness and the energetic tools that accompany it can change anyone's life, if they are choosing. Add that to people in 170-something countries taking part—and what you get is the possibility of consciousness changing the whole planet. Hooray!

May I say thank you for my wedgie, Gary! Although it took over three years, I actually got it—and now I can say, "Yes, Gary, I am *great*." (And there's no "but" at the end of that sentence!)

And then there's Dr. Dain Heer. Even when he comes from his potency, Dain has so much sweetness and caring that you want to jump into his arms, feel safe and choose to change. Because you so deeply know how much he desires that for you, it ignites that same energy in you. In *Monsters of Magic*, one of the most amazing Access classes he facilitates, I found a place so deeply buried within me that now demanded nothing less than BEing whatever the fuck it takes to have all of ME now.

How can it get even better than that? I'd experienced years and years of energy work when Dain worked on my body. Something very different occurred. My body began to receive in a way it had never allowed before. Or maybe it was me allowing my body to receive. Either way, that session has created a way for me to be in communion with my body and allow so much more.

Together, Gary and Dain are a dynamic duo. They are the Batman and Robin of consciousness and they are changing the world.

For me, Gary and Dain are HOME.

If this book could be the contribution to invite someone into the world of these two amazing men, then I will consider it a success.

WHATEVER THE FUCK IT TAKES

Never give in.

Never give up.

Never quit.*

These words are the motto of Gary Douglas and Access Consciousness®.

Access Consciousness® Tools for being the most powerful, magical and inconceivable YOU you can be.

By Barbra Gilman
with Madeleine Eno

© 2018 Barbra Gilman

ACCESS
CONSCIOUSNESS®
PUBLISHING

Whatever the Fuck It Takes

Copyright © 2018 by Barbra Gilman

ISBN: 978-1-63493-154-0

Published by:

Access Consciousness Publishing, LLC

www.accessconsciousnesspublishing.com

Printed in the United States of America

1st Edition

Contents

Introduction

As you can probably tell from the title, in this book I'm going to use the word "fuck."

Some people won't mind. Some will. If this word bothers you, let me ask you something: What if the word "fuck" was the **magic wand** that could catalyze you to open the door to *everything* you've always known you really are?

I know this about you: Even while people were judging you as weird, nutty, different and wrong, you knew there was something inside of you that was powerful and could possibly even change the world, if only you could access it. If only you could get there.

However, no matter how many books you read or courses you took, it remained so deeply hidden that you wondered if there really was a "there" and if you would ever find it.

Well, as they say, I've "been there, done that!" I get it! If you're really ready to start choosing *for* you and not *against* you, read this book. I guarantee you won't have to take nearly as long as it took me to get there.

If you're ready to receive, this is my gift to you.

The gift of you Being YOU!

Being infinite, potent, powerful and inconceivable.

Being the POSSIBILITY of the YOU you know you are here to BE.

Now…if you had all this, would that word "fuck" still bother you?

Are you really going to let a single, small word stand between you and infinite possibility?

No?

Good!

I have to admit that the only time I'd use the word before I came to Access Consciousness® was if I spilled a glass of red wine on a white sofa. "Oh, fuck!"

Now I choose to use it at much more meaningful times: Like when I'm facilitating a class or working with clients and their resistance comes up. That's usually when the possibility of change is right there— the door to everything that they've been asking for.

At that moment, though, the personality is fighting to keep the limitation in place, while the being that they truly are is panting like a dog that hasn't had water in days, demanding "right here and now please!"

Believe it or not, **fuck is the magic wand** that opens the door.

As soon as I go into this energy and use "fuck," it busts all that resistance apart. The closed doors magically open. I'm not talking to the person via the "role" they created to fit in anymore; I'm addressing the energy—a place that they don't even know exists yet. And they allow the energy to be released and the change to take place.

That is the potency and magic of FUCK.

And that's what this book is about—unleashing YOUR potency and magic.

The word is plenty on its own, but I've also got a great acronym for it: *Furthering Unlimited Conscious Knowing!*

And I've also heard that centuries ago in England the word stood for "Fornication Under Consent of the King." Back in the day it was supposedly used as a permit granting a couple permission to copulate in order to create a child. The permit with the abbreviation "FUCK" would be placed on the couple's door.

And if that isn't a form of creation energy I don't know what is! Crazy, right?

If you're really ready to begin creating change in your life, please be in total allowance of this word.

And for anyone still having a hard time with it, here's a fun exercise to change the energy around the word: Just say it fast five times in a row before you read on!

That usually puts a smile on the face of even my most resistant student.

I wrote this book as an invitation for you to choose these possibilities:

- To stop giving up you so you can fit in.
- To be willing to be inconceivable.
- To choose for you and not against you.
- To be willing to receive judgment and not run from it.
- To no longer cut off pieces of you so others don't have to feel less than.

- To be willing to show up as the potent bitch you truly be (as required) — the one who changes the world.

- To no longer give up your Wonder Woman being when you're with a man just so he doesn't feel less-than...all the while knowing how to manipulate so he feels as big and great as he "needs" to. (Whew!)

- To take off that fucking pathetic suit and burn it!

- To be the GIFT and INVITATION to your community and your children so they can show up BEing and doing the same — and changing the world!

So, if being any of these sounds good to you, just consider FUCK the power and potency that you be that you pretend not to be so you'll never be as inconceivable as you truly BE!

Got it? Good. Let's dive in.

* If you happen to be a guy and pick up this book, it's just as much for you. And if you actually read it...well, let me tell you, you're an amazing guy!

Glossary of Terms

Access Consciousness®: Access Consciousness® is a set of tools and processes designed to facilitate more consciousness for everyone. The invitation of Access is to help you acknowledge you as the infinite being you truly are and to step into generating a life beyond what you think you are. Access Consciousness® is designed to help you Further Unlimited Conscious Knowing!

The Access Clearing Statement®: The clearing statement is like a magic wand that takes away what you're willing to let go of. Have you ever wanted to change things just by asking them to change? Well, using the clearing statement is how you do that. It's designed to bring up energies that hold the limitation and clear them. When you read the clearing statement, you'll see it's in the first person.

When I work with clients or teach classes, I ask questions followed by the clearing statement—and that's what I've done in this book. The purpose of the question is to bring up the energy of a certain limitation. For instance, "What is right about this that I'm not getting?" As you read it, you'll actually be releasing the energy that creates a limitation. What it clears is everything that holds that limitation of you as wrong (and it might have been there for trillions of years). Now, the door is open. It's like there's a bee in your house you can't find, and all you do is say a magic word. Suddenly the bee comes out and you know exactly what to do with it.

Another way to think about it: The clearing statement is like a vacuum, sucking up as much of the energy of it you are willing to let go of. (And that means all of the conclusions, decisions and limited points of view that have been holding it in place.)

The full clearing statement sounds a little wild. It goes like this:

Right Wrong, Good Bad, POD POC, All Nine, Shorts, Boys and Beyonds®

In the book, I've shortened it to POD POC—and that's all you need to say! The magic is all there.*

By the way, you'll see that we use the word "destroy" in the questions. This bothers some people. Remember, though, you can't have creation without destruction, and what's being destroyed here is simply *limitation*. And while we're at it, "uncreating" is another word that confuses folks. Imagine if you'd never bought the lie of that limitation in the first place—your life would be totally different. You're destroying and uncreating all the decisions, limitation and points of view that are holding you back—and there's nothing to be afraid of in this language. The clearing statement doesn't take away *anything* that's working for you—it's taking away limitation so you have a greater possibility.

Humanoid: There are two kinds of beings in the world: humans and humanoids. Humans are the ones who don't look for other possibilities as they attempt to maintain the status quo. "Two things are certain: taxes and death" is a human point of view. With humans, there's a lot of judgment of others and things move very slowly.

---

* *If you happen to be a guy and pick up this book, it's just as much for you. And if you actually read it...well, let me tell you, you're an amazing guy!*

Humanoids are the opposite. They judge *themselves* and from the time they're small feel like they don't fit in. They look for ways to make things better and try to change the status quo. In Access Consciousness they say, "If you know there is more to life but don't know where or how to find it, you may be a humanoid."

Hundredth Monkey Effect: In 1979, biologist Lyall Watson published *Lifetide,* the story of a monkey tribe on an island near Japan. In the book he tells how a vast amount of freshly dug sweet potatoes, a new food for the monkeys, was dumped on the island and became covered in sand. The monkeys were not too excited about eating the dirty potatoes. However, one bright monkey solved the problem by taking the potatoes down to the water and washing them off. One by one the other monkeys started to do the same. When about 100 monkeys had acquired this knowledge, other monkeys on other islands, completely separate from the original monkeys, started washing their potatoes, too.

The **hundredth monkey effect** is a phenomenon in which a new behavior or idea is claimed to spread rapidly by unexplained means from one group to all related groups once a critical number of members of one group exhibit the new behavior or acknowledge the new idea.

Insane Asylum: We live in a lie—very much like the one depicted in the movie, *The Truman Show*—and we believe that it's real. To me, our world is more like an insane asylum. The term is my humorous way of describing the craziness of a reality that is actually based on a lie—yet everyone believes it's real. Think about the children's tale, *The Emperor's New Clothes,* and you'll get what I mean.

BE-ing: You'll soon see I use the word BE (in capital letters) in places where it's not typically used. For instance, I'll say, "who you truly BE" instead of "who you truly are." That's because "are" represents doing. You're *doing* to prove you're *being* because of the lie you're buying. Make sense?

Try this: Doing is not really you. It's the role, character and costume you've taken on to follow the orders of this reality. BEing, however, is you showing up as YOU, the infinite being, with all your awareness, knowing and magic — living in the moment and choosing for YOU!

Knowing (vs. Thinking): Early on, we are taught to think and that all the value we can offer is in our thinking. Which is quicker, though, thinking or knowing? Answer: Knowing. An infinite being just *knows*. You are an infinite being. You are energy. You simply *pretend* that you don't know what you really know in order to keep yourself small — to fit in and not be judged.

Tools: Many people don't get that Access Consciousness® tools are real until they start using them. Even though all of the tools here may seem simple or childish, please do not pass over them! Don't buy the lie that it has to be difficult — the tools of Access® are simple and playful. And they will change your life, IF YOU USE THEM![1]

---

[1] To learn more about the Access clearing statement®, check out what Dr. Dain Heer has to say (www.theclearingstatement.com). Find some recorded versions at www.barbragilman.com.

Chapter 1

WAKE UP TO THE LIE

Consider this your wake-up call.

The GREATEST gift you can give yourself is to be YOU — never, ever, EVER giving you up, for anyone or anything!

What would it take for you to be willing to BE whatever the fuck it takes to simply be YOU?

Consider yourself advised that BEing you may look a little different than you might expect it to look.

It's not a to-do list or a meditation or a mantra. It's not a cult or a religion or an instruction manual. I hope you keep reading anyway. Because being your most potent and powerful self requires waking up to the lie of you.

I have a knowing that if you picked up this book, you are choosing YOU and you are ready for the journey.

And I also have a knowing that you are here to be a contribution and an invitation of consciousness to others and together create change on the planet!

However, first things first.

Ask yourself this question:

What do I know down-deep that I can be — that I've been pretending not to be, that if I would be it, would change everything in my world?

Are you believing the lies, inventions and fantasies instead of living your life and choosing for YOU? Do you continue making yourself wrong, all the time?

Here's the thing. The greatest pain you can experience in the world is knowing deep down who you are and not BEing that. Trust me, I am very familiar with this one!

So much of how you show up in your life is based on the LIES, inventions and fantasies that have been impelled on you, then you buy them and, guess what? They are now yours!

These lies, inventions and fantasies become your truths.

It's like you're slipping into a Halloween costume, every single day.

Each day, you are believing:

- that you are limited, small, impotent or powerless — that you are wrong.
- that you are too old, too poor, too tired or too late.
- that joy, ease and happiness are impossible.

These are not the truth — these are lies and inventions.

If I undefined and dissolved me as I've been pretending to be, what is it that I would truly be and could choose to be, that I think that I'm not?

Everything that is, I now destroy and uncreate. POD POC.

You've Always Felt So Different

As I said earlier, I know a few things about you already.

- You've felt like a bit of a weirdo since you were little, and have marched to the beat of a very different drummer.

- You never quite understood how to "toe the line" at school or work, or it was just too boring and you always felt like you required a change, or you kept getting fired! (Am I right?)

- You always blame yourself for being pathetic or wrong when things go sideways. You rarely blame other people.

- You feel like there may have been a time when you were in touch with your awareness — or what you might call your inner guidance — however it's been too long and you just don't know how to do that anymore. Or it might seem like your inner guide is speaking a different language than you are.

- And you always have known you were here to do something great. You had this feeling the "Great You" was somewhere out there — waiting for you to catch up.

Right?

I know because all of these were true for me, too.

What has happened to you and me is that we simply bought the lie of the world because we turned off our own inner GPS.

What? You didn't know you had a GPS system?

So really, do you think that the universe...consciousness...omnipotent creator of all *might* have come up with a GPS system before the Department of Defense invented it in the 1970s?

Actually, the universe installed in each of us our very own, personal GPS system.

OK, now, calm down. I know you're excited to hear more.

So here it is....

We are all created with the same energy, yet each one of us has one unique speck of energy that sets us apart from everyone else. When I talk about "the difference that you BE," this is what I'm talking about.

When you follow that energy—that is, if you get a chance to know that following it is even possible—it is incredible. It's as if your whole life becomes like walking into the Grand Mall of Possibilities as the doors magically open before you—without any pushing or struggling.

The thing is, our GPS gets turned off—usually when we're quite young. Once that occurs we don't feel whole. We have that lost feeling most of us experience as we seek the lie that is being perpetrated on us. Why does this happen, you ask?

Because we are taught to be perfect, right, and good little girls and boys and to listen to what we are told. We believe the lies, inventions and fantasies. Why wouldn't we? It's the formula that we are fed from Day One, here in the insane asylum.

The thing is, whatever we seek—whether it's a mate or a career or a house or a Maserati—can never make us feel whole. Never! No matter how much we think it will. There always seems to be something missing, because we are not BEing who we really are! Does that make sense?

You have spent your entire life trying to prove that you are not what you never were!

What have I made so vital, valuable and real about the artificial reality of this world that requires me to lessen my magic in order to be here?

Everything that is, I now destroy and uncreate. POD POC.

So why would we turn off our GPS system if it's so vital, valuable and real?

Well, most children come into the world being very loved and nurtured. (Most…I know not all of them do.) And, when you get down to it, what does an infant really require? In the beginning, there's not that much to do. Parents give the bottle or breast, bathe the baby and change the diaper. (Yes, I know some of them are poopy — and I know the parents might be bleary-eyed!) Anyway, at this point the child feels only wonderful energy of nurturing and caring — and they are received for who they BE. Lo and behold, the GPS system they were born with is intact.

In every child's life, however, comes the defining moment when that wonderful energy changes and the GPS system switches off.

Here's how it happens….

Picture a cute toddler happily sitting in her high chair. Mom serves her a plate of spaghetti and meatballs with lots of sauce. Now, the little girl has just started playing with gravity. She sees a "ball" on her plate. Of course, she throws it to see what will happen. And the tomato-sauce covered meatball hits Mom's new designer wallpaper.

Mom blows up. "My new wallpaper! It's ruined! Look what you did!" She loses it. And so does the baby girl. Her world has changed dramatically. The cooing and loving has turned to anger and wrongness.

The little girl decides she is wrong. In the very moment she was being her pure self, she did something wrong to anger Mom. She forms a conclusion and makes a decision that being ME and playful is a wrongness that gets me *that* energy. Therefore, I am never going to be me and allow *that* energy to happen again. She starts to cut off pieces of herself, thinking, if I am too playful, if I am being ME, this will happen again.

Let's join our little girl a few years later. She loves to sing. She's discovered her voice. She feels so happy when she belts out a tune and her parents clap and praise her for her beautiful voice.

However, her mother also experiences migraines. One day, Mom is in bed with a terrible headache. The girl, as usual, begins to sing as she plays in her room. Mom, in her pain and desperation, yells out for the girl to stop: "Quiet! All that awful noise is hurting my head!"

Once again, the girl makes a decision that who she is is wrong. And she cuts off yet more pieces of herself.

She could have been the next Adele. However, she gave up herself to fit in and be right and be the perfect little girl so Mommy would love her again. She cut herself off from her GPS system. She bought the lie that she was wrong.

You have been doing that for eons—giving YOU up. Cutting parts of yourself off to never be "wrong" again. And in that moment that you give up you, your GPS system shuts down.

The good news is you can re-start your GPS system. However, the GPS system is for the "real you."

And I have to tell you, the "real you" is someone you don't even have a clue about. Yet. Because the greatness, the creator, the magician you truly BE has been kept from you and taken from you by the lie you bought.

From the time of your defining moment—like our little girl's moment in the high chair—you have been living a lie. You've been living an invention of the Not You.

What energy can my body and I be to generate, create and actualize a fantastic, amazing, unreal, unbelievable, phenomenal, magical reality with total ease?

Everything that is, I now destroy and uncreate. POD POC.

How amazing would it be to have your GPS system back?

Everywhere I've been living lost in the past of my life, claiming the disappointment and the wrongness of me....

Everything that is, I now destroy and uncreate. POD POC.

When I was young I was pure magic. Almost everything I asked for would appear. My GPS system was alive and well into my young adulthood. Magic is what I was…until I bought into others' judgements.

Many years ago, when my daughter was an infant, we were heading out to visit friends with her. It was very cold and I wanted the baby and me to be warm. My husband came up with my beautiful fur coat to put it on me and I said, "No, I'm not wearing it tonight!"

He said, "Why wouldn't you wear it? It'll keep you so warm."

I told him our friends were envious. I knew their judgment was going to be palpable and I didn't want to see my girlfriend's face when I walked up in that coat.

He couldn't believe it and thought I was over-reacting, so I wore it and I told him to watch her face — to be aware. Sure enough, when she opened the door every part of her being changed energetically. Her smile collapsed into a frown as she spotted me in the coat. Her shoulders noticeably slumped. My husband shot a look at me with his eyes popped out — acknowledging the moment I'd predicted. What I see now when I look back at this moment is that I was willing to give up my gift of magic and creation — just so she wouldn't judge me. I was actually turning off my GPS system!

Years later, after my divorce was final and I had lost a lot of those nice things, I raised my hands to the universe and said, "Good! Now I have nothing for people to be jealous about."

Oy! Talk about language creating reality. From that moment on, my amazing gift of magic diminished. And I tried to navigate without my GPS working.

How I Dug out of the Lie

What happens when we keep buying the lie like our little "Adele" did is that we end up feeling not good enough, wrong and pathetic. We start to energetically create an energy like this: "I can't…I'm wrong and pathetic and might as well kill myself."

Killing yourself can take all kinds of forms, and it's always about lowering the vibration of the body. Killing yourself can be: Numbing out. Checking out. Consumerism. Drugs. Doing-Doing-Doing. (You know what doo-doo is, right?)

This reality we live in (what I call the "insane asylum") is really good at capturing our attention to keep us busy enough that we never get to know what's *really* going on or who we *truly* BE.

Most people live life buried in the lie, certain that it's the truth.

Let me pause here and explain what the "lie" is. The lie is everywhere that you've bought the wrongness and "less-than" and "pathetic" of you.

Being the greatness of you means digging out of the lie you've been believing all this time. As Dr. Dain Heer would say, "It's like digging through enough shit so you can find the pony!"

What if you're not as fucked up as you think you are? What if you being YOU is the magic that creates possibility and choices that can change *everything*?

From the time I was small, I knew I was really different from other kids. In my family, I actually felt like I was the adult and my parents were the children. I would only show my cute and loving "character" or role—while I hid my deep knowing and awareness because no one got it. It's not that I cared about being different or that I couldn't hide. It just wasn't fun for me. My saving grace in life has been that I love being different.

I was aware. I also was hip to the fact that so much of what was happening around me was a lie. And I could tell immediately when others believed those lies.

Because I acted "woo-woo" before woo-woo was even a thing, my schoolmates would say things like, "Hey, Barbra, when's your spaceship coming to get you?" The good news was I always had a couple of friends who arrived on the same spaceship!

I had a very good sense back then of who I was. My inner GPS system was very intact and I knew I could create magic!

Yes, I've always been pretty "out there" and definitely different! I've been in five major relationships. I've lived large, traveled and lived abroad, spoken on large stages, and hung out with some very amazing and impressive people—from business moguls and movie stars to gurus, royals and quantum physicists. I've worked with incredibly powerful healers and met the people that you've seen interviewed by Barbara Walters, Jesse Ventura, 60 Minutes or Rachel Maddow.

I've always played at the "work" I love—whether I was designing Manhattan apartments or upstate country homes when I was young or facilitating the parenting program I created, writing my books, working with Neale Donald Walsh, contributing to the *Indigo* books or assisting people to be all they could be by choosing consciousness. If you asked them about me years ago, my friends and clients might have said I was "out there" and "different." I prefer the word "conscious," however it was not used much back then—even now most people don't know what it really means.

Just a few months ago a very lovely woman I know watched a video of me facilitating an Access® Intro class. She said, "Barbra, I adore you, but I have no idea what you're talking about. I always thought that if your eyes were open, you were conscious!"

Even though I've been branded with titles like Transformational Specialist, Life Muse and Quick-Change Artist, and have assisted people to make profound shifts in their lives, I've felt like a "closet person" for most of my life. Despite all this work I was doing in the world it was like the real me was tucked away and I didn't know how to find her.

I was buying the lie. As open, out there and conscious I thought I was, I didn't really have ME.

What have I made so vital, valuable and real about the lie of me, that never gets me to acknowledge, claim and own the gift of me?

Everything that is, I now destroy and uncreate. POD POC.

The thing is, for a long time what I wanted way more than consciousness was the role, the character and the costume of the fantasy I was looking for. My parents had treated me like a true Jewish princess — and I totally wanted to be that princess. Honestly, I didn't care so much about the Jewish part — just give me the fabulous lifestyle! (Jewish, Christian, Buddhist — that didn't matter to me. I knew that religion was the greatest separator of mankind from way back!)

And more often than not throughout my life, I was the princess. I loved everything that came with that title: clothes, cars, huge houses, shopping on a whim at Saks and Bloomingdales.

However, no matter how much I had or bought or was given, it was never enough. The problem was that I was trying to create a fantasy. And by definition, this is not real.

Growing up as I did in New York City, I'd bought the fantasy lock, stock and barrel — and did a great job perpetrating it on myself! No matter what beautiful material objects I had, no matter what man came in and took the place of the loving Daddy who had bought me whatever I wanted, there was still something missing.

Back then I didn't know what it was. Now I do.

What have I defined as the parameters of my life that keeps me from creating something greater?

Everything that is, I now destroy and uncreate. POD POC.

What was missing was the REAL ME.

Not that I wasn't pursuing a spiritual path all this time. Starting in my late teens I took every kind of self-growth and spiritual course I could and learned all the healing modalities the minute they came on the scene. (Mind you, I also had the fabulous homes, the summers in the Hamptons and the shopping excursions at Bloomingdales, too.)

About nine years ago, my course changed dramatically, though I didn't realize it for quite a while. I had a reading with a South American healer who'd been recommended by my former partner's millionaire client. Very few people got to work with this man. He worked in the energetic realms and he could tell if anyone or anything was trying to stop or limit you.

At the end of our session he told me something I'll never forget: "You are never really being YOU." While I understood the words he was using, I didn't have a clue what he was really telling me!

He looked at my website and read my bio to me using a funny, judgmental kind of voice, almost mocking me! What? Why!? I listened to the recording over and over again. I tried to look at it from every direction I could conceive of. I couldn't get at what he was trying to convey.

Because the lie was in the way.

It wasn't until about two years ago — more than five years after the reading — that I got it. He was trying to tell me that I was caught up in the *structure* of the perfect and right me, rather than just BEing the real ME. I now have much more of the ME that he was talking about and am still asking for more, better, greater!

And that happened thanks to the incredible work of Access Consciousness®. I was finally out of the lie.

Today, consciousness is my ice cream. It's my joy and my reason for being. I know what I'm here to BE, which is the same thing that I've done my whole entire life. I just happen to use the Rolls-Royce of tools now–I can be an invitation for what's possible when one is choosing consciousness.

I arrived at this place because I was finally willing and choosing to BE and do whatever the fuck it takes to BE and have all of me!

And now, in those times that I forget and open the door to the insane asylum again (I'll explain a lot more about that in Action 3), I don't make myself wrong, at least not for more than a few minutes!

To reactivate my GPS, I simply ask:

What can I BE and do different to change this, with ease?

That's how it has gone for me and that's how it goes for everyone destined to experience consciousness — to some degree or other. The Universe and the YOU that you haven't acknowledged yet have been prodding you to step into BEing who you really are.

So, the $100,000 question is:

Are you willing to do whatever the FUCK it takes to be YOU?

What would it take for me to be willing to do whatever the fuck it takes to have all of me?

Everything that is, I now destroy and uncreate. POD POC.

To those of you who know you chose to come here to be one of the 100 monkeys, those who know that you are here so the planet has a chance to survive, and those who will not let the draw of the ordinary pull you any longer….

You are willing to take my invitation.

You are willing to keep showing up.

You are willing to do whatever the fuck it takes!

Yay, YOU!

What have I made so vital, valuable and real about the reality of everybody else's reality that keeps me choosing the non-magical, un-magical, anti-magical world I came here to change?

Everything that is, I now destroy and uncreate. POD POC.

What have I made so vital, valuable and real about living in a NO-CHOICE universe that keeps me from having a life that works for me?

Everything that is, I now destroy and uncreate. POD POC.

ACTION TOOL:
CHOICE (Your Personal GPS)

Let me make this clear,
the tool that trumps every tool is *choice*.
It's the greatest tool we have in the universe.
The thing is, most people think they have no choice. We are
taught from the beginning that we have no choice and we
don't deserve what we want.

Choice is a muscle — you have to learn how to use it.
And the choice has to be yours —
it doesn't come from others in the insane asylum.

So, when making a choice, ask yourself:

"If I choose this, would it be a contribution to my life?
To my body?
To my joy?"

Then, be aware of how it feels — heavy and contracted or
light and expansive.

Truth will always feel light and expansive.

That lightness is a green light for you to go ahead. A lie (for
you) will feel heavy and contracted. That's your red light.
STOP!

Do not pass "Go" until you ask more questions.

Chapter 2

BE WRONG AND STUPID...AND HAPPY

Here in the insane asylum, rightness is the drug of choice. What most people don't get, however, is that you have to go to WRONG to be right. And, the biggest fear we have (aside from death) is being *wrong*. We don't consciously know that is our fear. So being right, not wrong drives us, and we're not even aware of it.

And because we're so afraid of it, we use judgment to defend our rightness—we judge everything and everyone because we are simply so afraid of being wrong.

Everywhere I've decided, judged or concluded I will lose if I don't make the right choice, I now destroy and uncreate. POD POC.

Let me explain: You wouldn't be afraid of being wrong unless you'd bought the lie that you *could* be wrong. If you knew there wasn't such a thing as "wrong" and everything was just what it was in the moment...you would never use judgment again.

I'll say that one more time: Judgment is how you prove you're right. Let me ask you something: "Would you rather be RIGHT or happy?"

Judgment is the point of view someone takes to prove and defend the rightness of what they have chosen. It's vital to recognize the difference between *observation* and *judgment*. Usually judgment will have a contractive or heavy energy and observation will feel light and expansive. And anything that creates a judgment is also a judgment.

The Difference Between Judgment and Observation

Imagine you're walking down Broadway in New York City and get a craving for a piece of deliciously crispy New York style pizza. You ask a man on the street where you can find some good local pizza. He says, "Oh, go buy it from the fat guy on the corner."

Now, "fat guy" sounds like a judgment, right? Here's the difference: If it felt heavy and contractive when the man said it, yes, it was covered in judgment. However, if he used the word "fat" simply as a description and the energy was light, it would be an observation.

(By the way, if you happen to be reading this book and live in Portland, Oregon, circa 2018 and know where I can find a piece of some crispy New York pizza, please contact me! I'm dying for some!)

How to Shift from Judgment

One of my favorite tools to use when you want to shed judgment is called "Interesting Point of View" or what we in Access call "IPOV."

When you or someone else judges or says anything that has that heavy, contractive feeling—or when you have a thought that feels like that, say, "*Interesting point of view—I have this point of view. Isn't it interesting that I have this point of view that the pizza guy is fat….*" (or whatever judgment you're noticing). Keep repeating it until the energy has changed. And it will! This tool creates a greater space of no judgment for you to function and

ACTION TOOL:
INTERESTING POINT OF VIEW (IPOV)

Whenever a judgmental thought rises up, keep repeating:

"Interesting point of view, I have this point of view."

Isn't it interesting that I have the POV that....

[this person/situation should show up
any differently than the way they are!]

create from. Believe me, it's way more fun and light and expansive to be in this energy.

Try it on whatever is happening that you are judging right now: Isn't it interesting that I have the point of view that my tire should not be flat or that my husband should take out the garbage or that my child should only get As?

If you have the POV that *anything* going on in your life should be different than the way it's showing up, you're judging it as wrong—which takes away the ease in your life. And definitely creates the trauma and drama. Remember, our fear of being wrong is driving us without us knowing it. So powerfully!

This tool is your BRIDGE.

So, if you are having a judgment that something is wrong—maybe your boss told you to work late or you just ran out of gas. You think you have to judge it as bad, wrong, pathetic, etc. However, when you're in that place of wrongness, is your life going to work well? Are you going to have ease or will you be in the trauma and drama?

Are you a little kid stomping your feet in a temper tantrum at whatever just happened? What will that create? The energy you experience now will create, oh, yeah! the rest of your life. Why not make it amazing? Why not make it fun?

How much trauma and drama am I using to create the exile of me that I'm choosing?

Everything that is, I now destroy and uncreate. POD POC.

Let me give you another example:

You're on your way to a big job interview. You're broke and you really need this job, you're all dressed up and you're ready to nail this interview. On your drive, you get a flat tire. And it starts raining. Now you're going to be late. In that nanosecond, you make it wrong. You're upset at you — you're judging it: "Shit, this is horrible! I'm screwed!" Enter fear. Scarcity. Anger. You're dripping wet. You kick the tire. When you call a tow truck they say it will be an hour until they can get there. You miss the interview.

When you're in judgment like this, you're way out of awareness. At the same time, you're cutting off the possibility for anything that does not match the judgment—which would be anything wonderful—to show up.

Lo and behold, your day gets even worse. When you call to tell the company what happened, the human resources person tells you they will not reschedule your interview. The tow truck driver charges you $75 to change your tire. Your new shoes are ruined. You feel pathetic and wrong and go from panic, anger and fear into total despair.

You've probably had a day like that when things went from bad to worse. Oh, my God, if you haven't, I'd love to meet you!

When you use **IPOV,** however, it brings you into allowance. You allow magic to happen.

Isn't it interesting that I feel I have to control and judge everything and if it doesn't show up the way I think it should — which would be a result...and results are always based on the past, by the way—and negates all possibility of anything better showing up?

When you use the magic tool of **IPOV,** there's a whole new possibility of what could show up.

Let's look at the same story from another angle:

You get the flat tire. You go into a trauma-drama temper tantrum for a minute and then you remember your tools. You say, "Interesting Point of View, I Have This Point of View... Isn't it interesting that I am concluding and deciding that the flat tire is wrong and bad. Isn't it interesting that I am concluding that everything I want is now gone."

And as soon as you say it, the energy starts to dissipate. It takes you out of trauma, drama, fear and judgment of what's happening being wrong. And voila! You are no longer deathly afraid of being WRONG.

Back to the side of the road: All of a sudden, a truck stops for you. A lovely young man gets out and starts helping you with your tire. You share the story of your interview. He asks, "What kind of job was it?" You tell him. And he says, "Wow, my father has a company just like that. I'll introduce you to him." In the end, you get a job with the father's company that you love and that pays twice as much as the one you were interviewing for.

Let's look at another scenario. (I want you to really get this!)

You walk into the kitchen after a busy day and find the mess your children left on the kitchen counter and see the overflowing trash can. You get very angry. Why are you the one left to clean this up? Your husband is supposed to clean up after the kids and take out the trash! Why doesn't he do it? You worked all day and already cleaned up the breakfast dishes... You just wanted a moment to yourself tonight! You start slamming dishes around because this just sucks!

Let's replay the scenario. You're able to interrupt the momentary rant and remember to use the tool:

Interesting Point of View, I Have This Point of View:

Wow, isn't it interesting that I believe that my husband has to clean up the kids' mess and take out the garbage?

Suddenly, you see that you're making your husband responsible for your happiness in this moment. When you do IPOV, the energy settles and you see another possibility. You can look at this situation and say, "Hmm, what if this is actually MY issue?"

Then the possibility appears: "What if I just clean the mess and take out the garbage and that's that. It'll take two minutes—no big deal! Then I can go read my book for a few minutes."

How much judgment am I using to resist and refuse the peace, ease and joy I could be choosing?

Everything that is, I now destroy and uncreate. POD POC.

The truth is you're the one who's concerned—you're the one whose problem it is. If you get that you can clean it up, then the garbage is gone and you're not angry at your husband. And maybe, from that change in you, he starts feeling great and asks you out to dinner. You have a lovely night together and the situation is 180-degrees different than it would have been had you let loose on him and the kids.

To really get the most of this tool, you want to use it for every thought and feeling— even the positive ones. Yes, the positive ones! Say **IPOV** for every thought and feeling you have for a month and your life will change. Or start with just a week... You'll start to see a change and you'll want to keep going for a month!

What if whatever is going on in the moment—the dirty dishes or the difficult boss or the flat tire—is the gift that you haven't acknowledged, that if you did acknowledge, could change your entire life?

What if you could look at it without judgment, functioning from the space of "Interesting point of view — I have the point of view that what just occurred makes me wrong."

The wonderful thing about IPOV is that you're choosing to BE the space of total allowance where judgment does not exist. Talk about changing your life!

The Lesson of the Lady in Pajamas

When I learned about this tool, I loved it. I saw its potency right away. So I was rigorous in watching out for my judgments and noticing where I made myself and others wrong (although, like you, I usually judged me much more than I judged others). One day, I was walking down the street in my lovely, upstate New York town, and noticed a woman walking toward me wearing pajamas and fuzzy slippers.

I was still in my Princess mode and thought WTF? She's wearing slippers and pjs in the street? In the middle of the day? Is she crazy? As soon as these thoughts came into my head, my hand flew to my mouth. *OMG, I'm judging her so much! I can't believe it!*

So I started **IPOV** right away. Isn't this interesting that I'm judging her for wearing this in the street? Actually, it looks like a very comfortable outfit — and those slippers look so cozy! Maybe I'll try wearing my pjs next time I come into town! I shifted that judgment right away.

Then, that very same week I went to a gathering at a private home. I walked into the living room, now in my fabulous designer role, and thought, "OMG, how ugly!" I astonished myself. *Oh my God! I'm doing it again!* So once again, I used my tool: Interesting that I have this point of view that everyone's house should be photo-ready for *Architectural Digest*!

When you function from this space, which, by the way, is called *allowance*, you're no longer living in the energy of judgment.

You're living in the energy of consciousness, which gives you the knowing to ask the question, "Is this really working for me?" Which creates the awareness of "definitely not!" Which creates the possibility of **IPOV.** Which can be the **contribution to change your entire life!**

Consciousness is receiving *everything* with no point of view. Total allowance.

As you can see from my examples, consciousness takes awareness. Lots of it. And more than that, it takes the willingness to be wrong. (That doesn't mean you HAVE to be wrong… you might simply be "mistaken" for a moment.) The cool thing is that when you're willing to be wrong, it actually happens less!

So, here's an example of what willingness to be wrong looks like:

A dear friend, who just happens to be a clean fanatic, was visiting me recently from Florida. She's the kind who starts fluffing the pillows the moment you stand up. I was making my protein shakes and some powder fell onto the counter. She starts right away to breathe heavily, stressed by the mess. Now, I'm normally pretty tidy, however what I've noticed is that after a while of being with her I do things I never do on my own: I spill water, I forget to wash the bottom of the pan, I knock things over. My behavior changes just by being in that energy!

Have you ever had this happen with a person? It's pretty interesting. You've been entrained energetically to what they are expecting you to be, so guess what? You show up being the wrongness they're expecting. We are actually mimicking the energy they're holding, so we have to show up being wrong.

Talk about crazy, huh?

When you have people like that in your life, it's like you're giving up YOU to fit into their judgment of you. So you actually BE that judgment. You are giving them what they're waiting for!

They've already labeled you such and such (clumsy, untidy, late, etc.). You energetically pick it up and you BE that for them!

Here's an amazing question to put out to the universe—it will assist you in being willing to have no point of view about being wrong:

**What would it take for me to be as wrong
and stupid as I can be?
Everything that is, I now destroy and uncreate. POD POC.**

**What stupidity am I choosing to create
the judgments of me that I'm using?
Everything that is, I now destroy and uncreate. POD POC.**

Everything is possible when you're not afraid of being wrong.

I can't say it enough: **The fear of being wrong controls you and limits what could be possible in your life.** Because in every moment and in every nanosecond that you're afraid of being wrong, you judge where you're going, who you're with, what you look like, what you're saying, etc., to continually make sure you're *right*. Talk about working hard!

As the bumper sticker says, what you resist persists. It's like a dog is biting your tush and won't let go.

You can't have fun when you fear being wrong. If your friends are going to karaoke, you won't go because you think you have a horrible voice and are afraid your friends will judge you and laugh at you. The equation here is a lie, a projection, an invention and a conclusion that equal up to your decision not to go— and you miss out on what could've been a fun time with your friends. Ouch!

This fear of being wrong is the #1 immobilizer of humanity and keeps us stuck in the lie. If there's no such thing as wrong and, therefore, you can't ever be wrong, what could be possible? Well, maybe you're "mistaken" for a few moments and that passes and then you could actually choose to be happy! How cool would that be?

We've made being wrong like being in the coffin. Once you get in, you don't get out!

Everywhere I think that finding the rightness of me is the solution....

I now destroy and uncreate. POD POC.

Actually, if you're living in the fear of wrongness, *you might as well be dead...* Doesn't no play, no fun and all lies sound like death? I know you'd like to choose something different.

The great news is you can: If you'd willing to be wrong and stupid then you don't have to resist against all of this and you'll probably show up being wrong and stupid much less! And in those moments that you are mistaken, you can just use your wonderful IPOV tool and shift the energy. This is called "living" vs. "serving a life sentence" — allowing all the fun and the play and the creation.

The Insane Asylum and the Möbius Strip

Welcome to Planet Earth, what I like to call the insane asylum (because it's true and funny at the same time!) This is where we've been trained from a very young age to judge *everything*. Judging is a full-time job here and for most people there's no time left to even consider that there's another possibility.

We speak the language of judgment. Listen into a typical conversation at a party or small talk at a coffee shop. There is *nothing* in there that is not judgment. It reminds me of being in high school — and I wasn't "in" high school even when I was there! I did service for my teachers at lunchtime to get myself out of the cafeteria, which to me was the absolute worst!

Most people get stuck in judgment for their entire lifetime—in the disappointment and dissatisfaction and wrongness of not getting what they think they want. That becomes the *result* they keep perpetrating on themselves...that's abuse of self. That's violence against self. If they don't have the mate, the job, the house, the car...they are WRONG.

What have I made so vital, valuable and real about dissatisfaction, disappointment and self-abuse that proves I will never be as right and good as everyone else, ever?

Everything that is, I now destroy and uncreate. POD POC.

However, what they want is just a lie, invention and fantasy anyway, remember?

They judge what everyone else is (or has) as "better" and what they have as "wrong"—and they judge themselves as wrong. This way they will stay disappointed, miserable and pathetic.

That's why you feel so conflicted—one part of you wants to be the greatness you know you are—or the greatness you *hope* you are, since you haven't allowed yourself to get close enough to acknowledge it (yet). And one part of you clings to the familiar comfort zone of trauma, drama and judgment while you drive around in the best car that you can afford (or can't afford) on the Möbius strip called life!

Do you know what I mean by Möbius strip? Picture a strip of paper twisted into a figure 8, that makes you go around and around on that continuous surface without ever hitting an edge. It's named for the German mathematician who discovered it.

I see most people walking around on their personal, endless Möbius strip, head hung and shoulders bent under all the wrongness, disappointment and judgment they feel...They could be stepping right over a sparkling diamond bracelet on the pavement and not see it!

Think of the white picket fence or the skinny body or the amazing Prince Charming or whatever your own favorite version of the lie/invention/fantasy is. When you don't have it, you're wrong, disappointed and judging yourself. Right?

You bought the lie and you continue to create the fantasy/invention as the result you're looking for. Most of the world is stuck in that lie, moving around the curves of that Mobius strip — never getting off. Never seeing what's possible.

What have I made so vital, valuable and real about *results* that keeps me in the limitation of what's not possible and keeps me disappointed?

Everything that is, I now destroy and uncreate. POD POC.

However, if you choose to sit and watch TV every night, and if you choose to take advice from what I like to call the inmates in the asylum (rather than from your own awareness) and if you choose to stay stuck in the stories of what you think is happening in our world, you're never going to even come close to being who you really BE.

(By the way, I enjoy a night with a romantic comedy or an episode of *Grace and Frankie* as much as the next person. That's not what I'm talking about!)

To get unstuck and to start experiencing what functioning from consciousness would create for you, start showing up in each moment asking questions. It's fun, it's playful and it changes everything! See page 88 for more about the potency of asking questions and the back of the book for even more potent questions.

Here are some possibilities:

What else is possible?
What's right about me I'm not getting?
What choice can I choose that would create ease and clarity here?

What can I BE and do different that would change this with ease?

What can I choose that would be a contribution to my life?

What I finally learned through Access Consciousness® is that if you have a judgment about anything, you can never receive anything greater than the judgment!

If you have a judgment that work is hard to do and money is hard to get, then the possibility of work being playful and fun would never show up in your life. And money will never come to you easily.

I bet that's one you're going to choose to change quickly!

Imagine if there's a stinking, rotten fish in the kitchen. Nothing is going to change if you think all day about what to do with the fish, how to get rid of the smell and what you're going to eat instead. It's not about fixing or changing the problems like these in your life. (And it's not about the flat tire or the dirty dishes!)

Seriously, it's about changing the whole fucking world....starting with YOU!

There are very, very few people who are going to say, "Whatever the FUCK it takes, I'm going to choose ME!"

I'm one of them. I'm willing to be wrong, be stupid, and be (very) happy.

What do I know that I can be, that I can now invite into this world?

Everything that is, I now destroy and uncreate. POD POC.

Let me tell you how I got here.

Chapter 3

CLOSE THE BACK DOOR

So, there I am, living blissfully on my mountaintop with my partner — a man who also happens to be a very successful, spiritual and aware healer. Maybe 10 years into our life together, he tells me, "You're moving into the next phase of your astrological cycle."

"Interesting," I say. "And....?"

"You'll begin moving towards the outer world again. So get ready to start re-creating yourself!"

"What do you mean, recreate?" I asked. "What else would I do? Who else would I be? I'm going to go out and become a ballet dancer?"

Now, astrology is an **algorithm,** so I don't buy it 100 percent. (I'll explain that in another book, but suffice it to say, I know my choice trumps *everything*.) However, I was willing to look at what he was saying and at what that possibility could create.

I knew something inside me was ready to make itself known, at least to me in this moment, so I gave up my resistance. I started diving into my very large bag of tools: EFT, NLP, emotional code...I'll spare you the entire list. And, of course, my partner was also using his amazing energy healing skills with me.

While I didn't have the words of Access Consciousness® yet, I knew the energy of what I was essentially asking for:

What would it take for me to be all of ME!
What would it take for me to shut my back door
so I never give me up again?

One day someone told me about online programs they'd discovered where hundreds of people tuned in to hear speakers from the spirituality and metaphysics world. I am about the furthest thing from a techy person there is, so this was news to me!

I went to the website and signed up. I started listening and quickly realized that the things people were talking about were already outdated to me. Remember, I'd been at this game for more than 30 years already…(You know, been there — done that!)

One of my favorite spiritual mentors up to this point was an entity known as Lazaris. He was the Abraham Hicks of the 70s and 80s. He would channel to large audiences in a few cities around the country. This gave me an amazing introduction to energy and consciousness and had, unbeknownst to me, created the steppingstones that prepared me to receive Access Consciousness®.

When I received the emails describing upcoming speakers, I'd check in to get the energy of the speaker. I didn't end up listening to very many. However, one day, I read about a woman speaking on Access Consciousness®. I'd never heard of it, however, reading the email gave me the awareness that said, "LISTEN!" very loudly!

Now, here's the interesting thing. When the woman started to speak I did not resonate with her energy or her voice, yet I found what she was saying utterly fascinating. Then, when she said the clearing statement, my body and my being went wild. It stirred something so exciting, yet at the same time strangely familiar, in me.

"OMG, what is this?" I asked myself.

I immediately went to the Access Consciousness® website and bought some classes. Now, what happened next, I'll never forget. My best friend/former husband Jamie and I sat out on one of my decks listening to them, again and again. I actually cried! My very long journey had now delivered me to this place where I knew I was home!

While this is such an understatement, the energetic processing and the clearing statement rocked my world! I started to use these tools with my long-distance clients on our phone sessions.

Now I knew my clients very well. I knew where they were stuck and where they struggled. I was familiar with their patterns and habits: Mary moved like a duck, Gloria moved like a snail, and so on. When I used the clearing statement on them, they transformed from snails to galloping horses and flying birds! Their lives were changing. They were no longer mired in the muck.

All I could think was, "Oh, my God. What is this and how do I get more?"

What is that saying? One small step for Woman; one giant step for Womankind (and Mankind)? That's what it felt like. It felt like I had received just what I'd been asking for all my life—and it was potent enough to change the world.

So, of course, I found the closest Access Consciousness® Bars® class and dragged Jamie with me as his birthday present. When I say, "dragged," I mean he did NOT want to go. It was a huge growth opportunity for me when I learned later that his reluctance to attend is exactly what occurs with so many people who come into contact with Access Consciousness®. Their awareness expands out and actually starts to take the class and becomes aware of the huge change that is possible. It is so big and so expansive that it freaks them out, because it's so different from where they are and who they are being. It is inviting them to the possibility of being all they truly BE! Now, for many people that's much too inconceivable, because it means they'd no longer fit in with their herd.

Why Are We So Scared of Not Fitting In?

In our world, fitting in is the numero-uno thing to do. We've been trained very well to fit in, and fitting in here means to be right! So, we give ourselves up in order to validate everyone else's point of view, and we get to be right at the same time. And boy-oh-boy, when we fit in and are accepted and still get to be right, it's like a triple-header Yankees game and the annual Macy's Thankgiving Day Parade rolled into one!

The Value of Fitting In

Most people's lives are trauma, drama and struggle. What is the value of that? Well, the value is when you have these, you get to fit in. You get to be like everyone else. You don't have to be inconceivable because you're part of the herd. You don't have to worry about standing out or getting kicked out. That's the value of fitting in. And if you fit in, you also get to share. We love that concept. Unfortunately, when you share you have to bring yourself down to the lowest common denominator of what the person you're sharing with can receive. They can only receive 1 percent of what you're saying, so you have to bring yourself down to 1 percent of you. Talk about giving you up!

Unless, of course, you stand outside the insane asylum and look at the notion of "fitting in." Now from that vantage point you can see that those who want to fit in are actually choosing against themselves, and never get to be who they truly could be. If they were choosing for themselves, that would actually change everything and give them a life of ease, joy and glory®! Oh, well, no significance here and no making anyone wrong. They can always come back and try it again!

What have I made so vital, valuable and real about giving me up to validate everyone else's point of view?

Everything that is, I now destroy and uncreate. POD POC.

OK, back to my story....

The Bars® class was great. My body and I felt amazingly light and clear and I totally got what an amazing contribution this would be to all of my clients and the world. I knew that I would use it as my ongoing maintenance program of choice and I knew I would go on to teach others to do the same.

I was ready for my next possibility: The Foundation class. For me, this was just the steppingstone to get to "The Choice of Possibilities" class (which was called Level 1 at the time.) This class was taught by Gary Douglas, the founder of Access Consciousness®, to whom I had been listening on the online classes. I was so ready to meet him. I could hardly wait. I was like a kid on Christmas Eve waiting to hear Santa dropping down the chimney, wondering what gifts I would receive.

Somehow, I knew that this would be the thing that would totally change my life. It did!

Not only did both classes change my life, as they do for most who take them, there was also an added bonus. I'd spent my whole life pursuing what I didn't even have words for yet knew existed, and when I heard Gary Douglas speak in person, I felt like I'd found my native language. It was so comforting that I cried even more happy tears. I truly had arrived home!

I still thank the universe for Gary Douglas and Dr. Dain (who I met later), every single morning. My gratitude is not only for the change that Gary and Dain have contributed to my life (which is beyond huge) it is also for the change that has been created for the entire planet, and continues every day!

I finally got it. I felt like I had awakened from the deep sleep of my princess fantasy. I'd been making myself so wrong all those years. I'd been judging me for never having the full and complete version of my fantasy because right before it actualized it would fall apart, again and again. And the biggest joke was that I wasn't wrong at all—because a fantasy never materializes off-screen!

Eventually the lie I'd been living was smashed to smithereens.

Even though I'd always been a little bit "larger than life," I was keeping my true potency in the closet and settling for the lesser version of me so I wouldn't be as inconceivable as I could be. After all, I was the Jewish princess, always waiting for the next daddy to sweep in and take care of me. In that fantasy, I never had to spread my wings too far because the "Daddy" was always there to spread his wings around me and keep me safe. It would have been frightening to choose anything different and unknown—and yet I had no clue I was so scared. Looking back now it's almost as if I was drugged...Oh, right, I was! Isn't that what they do to the inmates in insane asylums?

It was like I had been walking along a pathway strewn with diamonds—and instead of noticing any of the treasures, I kept my eyes focused on all the piles of dog poop. I focused on my expectations and projections, which are always based on the past. And in my case those expectations were about how the fantasy would only be destroyed once again, as it had been before. And, yet I still chose the fantasy! I wanted a partner to love me; I wanted wealth, a beautiful home, travel…However, deep down I believed I couldn't have it.

I was always a very bright student. What I had learned in the insane asylum was that it would be easier to not choose for me, by giving up the possibility of what I could create if I chose it, than to actually choose it, get it and then lose it again. It would be easier for me to keep the Back Door open (more on that later). I was not at all ready or willing to do whatever the FUCK it took. That was definitely not part of the Jewish princess package. I wanted a guarantee of a life less painful. Can I see a show of hands in agreement, please, so I can be right!

You've got to remember that when you're looking at a fantasy— there is NO way it will turn out to be right or enough, because.... hello, it's a fantasy! I, like everyone else here, was entrained to look for what will not work. To search for evidence of my wrongness. Like a dog on the scent of a sausage!

The thing is when you function this way, you don't even get a sausage; all you end up with is a conclusion.

Everywhere I look for fantasies to justify why I can't receive, I now destroy and uncreate. POD POC.

And my conclusion was that I was limited, not good enough, and wrong. (Even being the wonderful person I always knew I was and even living the bold and different way I was living). The energy I was entrenched in from who knows how far back felt like an endless Mobius strip of having and losing, losing and having. With Access Consciousness® it was as if I suddenly had access to a Penthouse on the 30th floor — and I realized that I had been living in a 4th floor studio all this time.

I saw that I had created such a perfect fantasy of what a princess should look like, should have, should be and should do that Walt Disney himself would've wanted to shake my hand. And now it was very clear, too, that there was no way I could have it!

Ouch! Talk about painful. The reason I could never attain it wasn't because I didn't deserve it or want it; it was because it wasn't real. However, the moment I was willing to actually see that in total allowance with no judgment, I was set free! I could sit back and see the whole fantasy falling apart into pieces that were actually re-creating themselves into my next adventure, as I watched. Once I had that awareness, I didn't waste another moment. I saw the lie of the fantasy. So, I went for it — I shut my back door and took away that escape route I'd always relied on. (However, mind you, I still wanted the image of the princess lifestyle. I hadn't quite let that desire go.)

That was the beginning of my new life. I had found my language and it had given me clarity, where before it was only a glimpse of a blurring knowing off in the distance. As the pieces came together, the words followed. I was now able to facilitate the knowing I always had with other people.

If someone would have asked me then, "Barbra, what do want to get out of Access? What do you *really* want?"

I would have said I still wanted the beauty, the fun, and the adventure — however I didn't require the same level of total luxury I'd always fantasized about. It was coming through a different language. It felt so different. And, by the way, I'm not looking for a "result" here; I'm asking the universe for an energy — to BE that energy of ease, peace, joy and excitement.

Since then, I have met more and more people who are at the point of knowing it's all a lie, and are asking for something different to take them beyond it, even when they don't know they're asking.

Once I discovered Access Consciousness®, absorbing everything I could about it became the driving force and total joy in my life. Living in allowance creates a level of ease you can't know living in unconsciousness. I closed my back door, and now I'm locking it, one lock at a time!

What Does Closing the Back Door Look Like?

It looks like not believing or allowing the fantasies or the inventions made up by ourselves or others. Those lies that sneak up on me like thieves in the night…or the excuses, reasons or justifications for me to leave me and head right out through that back door to meet that thief in the night.

As I said at the beginning, there is no perfect way to live here. There is only life and how you BE with it. You could do violence and abuse to you, which is how most people live here — that is also known as unconsciousness. Or you could be in allowance of you and *however* you show up — that is consciousness.

Closing the back door looks like caring for, nurturing and receiving you. Being in allowance of you however you show up. When life doesn't go according to plans, you will still be caring, nurturing and receiving you. That is consciousness.

If it showed up *not* how you wanted it, you could ask, "How could it get any better?"

For me, it looks like this: Any extra money I have goes toward my Access classes. I gobble up and *live* every Access nugget that I take in. I don't watch the news or study any energy system that comes down the pike anymore. I focus on Access. I listen to the Access audios and my processes throughout the day and especially when I'm driving. Believe it or not, Portland has worse traffic than New York!

I travel to take as many trainings as I can. I choose for me by being aware and asking questions—about what I eat, what movies I see, how I exercise, what I do on the weekend and how I show up in the world. I facilitate Access Consciousness® material with all my clients and hold Bars® and Foundations classes (and whatever else is speaking to me), private sessions and Bars®/body process exchanges at my home. I offer teleclasses all over the country and private sessions by phone. I study with Gary and Dain. I use all the tools I am sharing in this book every single day. And I am attracting people who resonate with the principles of Access in Portland, where I live now. (A long way from Bloomingdales, right? I still love getting back to New York City whenever I can!)

Do I have it 100 percent? No! That would be another fantasy. Do I sometimes fall on my face? Sure. What I do have (most of the time) is allowance for me however I show up without having to judge and make me wrong.

I continue choosing to never give me up. Living on this planet, that is a daily choice. However, the beauty of Access is that there is absolutely nothing else out there that gives you the language of consciousness, the tools *and* the energy work. It is a complete system—and a system that continually changes and expands.

ACTION TOOL:
Who Does This Belong To?
Return to Sender

This is the tool you'll probably use the most. Because you're
constantly taking on others' energy, feelings, expectations,
fear, worries and day-to-day thoughts. Though they're
not your own, you take them on as your own.
This tool is incredibly potent.

For every thought, feeling, emotion you have, ask yourself,
"Who does this belong to?"
If it's not yours, it just goes away.
Say, "Return to sender, with consciousness."

Would you believe (I hope you do after you read this!) that 90
percent of everything you think and feel is not yours? Yes, you
read that correctly! I know this can sound preposterous the first
time you hear it. However, it's true. And the good news here is
that once you start playing with the **Return to Sender** tool, not
only will you believe me, you'll also get the added bonus of getting rid of most of the trauma and drama and unwanted feelings
you think are yours.

Think about it this way:

Would you sneak into a neighbor's hamper and put on their
dirty underwear??

No? Well, guess what? That's exactly what you do.

And in doing all this, in closing the back door, returning to sender, and removing most of the escape routes I used to have—my

life and awareness have changed in ways I could never have imagined.

Remember there is no destination; what we're looking for is More-Better-Greater-Different.

I know there is so much more ahead. I KNOW I don't want to leave this planet feeling like I never became the most POTENT version of me, or at least gave it my best shot. And I am sure you don't want to, either.

Are you ready to change?

Did I hear a YES?

Great!

Now, let's change.

And let's change our world while we're at it.

It starts with a question.

What have I made so vital, valuable and real about never acknowledging, owning, and claiming the greatness of me by leaving my Back Door open?

I now destroy and uncreate it all. POD POC.

What if your need to fit in is actually one of the greatest limitations to what you can be and create in and as your life?

Would you give up the desire to fit in?

Starting today, would you be willing to be what is unimaginable and inconceivable to everyone around you?

I love this question for how powerful it is to change your life. It's like throwing magic into the universe. It will create something greater. And when it does, acknowledge you, be in the energy of gratitude and ask:

What can I create from this that's even greater?
What is inconceivable to me that I'm not acknowledging,
that if I acknowledged it would set me free?

Everything that is, I now destroy and uncreate. POD POC.

ACTION TOOL:
Asking the Universe and Demanding of YOU
"1, 2, 3!"

When you've tried everything, things aren't changing,
and nothing seems to work —
you get to that energy of FUCK!
Do you know that energy?

You're saying: "Whatever the fuck it takes
this is going to change NOW!"
You're not fooling around anymore —
this is a demand you are making of YOU!
The universe always has your back when you're
choosing consciousness and choosing for you.

You have to BE that energy! This demand is for YOU! So
BE that energy and feel it in your whole body. Close your
palms, lift them up to in the air. Fling out your hands three
times as you say, "1!", "2!" and when you get to "3!"
open your palms forcefully.

"The universe always has my back.
It's already choosing for me.
I'm choosing change here and this is happening now!"

Chapter 4

MOVE OUT OF THE INSANE ASYLUM

Way back when the movie was popular, I used to say it was like we lived in "The Truman Show" in our world. If you haven't seen it (P.S. You should! It's on Netflix. Go watch it tonight!), it's about Truman, a man who was raised since infancy by a corporation. His whole life exists inside a simulated TV show, until he discovers what's going on. When things in our world got crazy years ago, I called it "The Truman Show on steroids." Now it's even crazier, so I just keep things simple and call it the "insane asylum."

We're living in a reality that is a lie. It's make-believe—an invention—a fantasy. And it's not like it's a fantasy that makes things work for us so we have a great life. No, it's an invention to keep us as limited, small and pathetic as possible....living crappily-happily ever after. They do such a good job at it that, just like everyone who lived in Truman's world, we believe it.

We all have our own versions of the lie that we live, too—from attitudes like "money can buy happiness" to the Cinderella dream that our prince is going to someday show up with his golden carriage and make everything perfect.

What we don't understand is that clinging to these beliefs has only created the mediocrity and fear that we all live in now. It has created the insane asylum. And to add to the craziness, we are so well programmed that we can't even see the lies any more. Not only did we accept them, we also educated ourselves in them, built our worlds around them defending them as the truth.

And now, the notion of coming face-to-face with the truth is more than a little painful and scary. Admitting that we made a mistake or that we—God forbid!—might be wrong, is difficult. One of the things about the insane asylum is that when we're in here, we're so terrified to be wrong. (Remember, being willing to be wrong is one of the most potent things you can do!)

By living so long at such an unconscious level we have created a wasteland of material addictions. We have lost touch with who we really are in the haze of pursuing a fantasy built on lies.

How It Goes in the Insane Asylum

In the insane asylum wives do not know who their husbands are, husbands don't have a clue who their wives are, parents can't figure out their own kids, and kids haven't got the foggiest idea who their own parents are. About the only place any of us experiences unconditional love (which is actually the state of "no judgment") is with our dogs or cats—or birds, lizards or hamsters, etc.

That condition of disconnection from everything and everyone who should matter to us doesn't just exist in our families. It extends out to our relationships with the earth. It contributes to a way of thinking that allows us to ruin our air, pollute our water, dump toxic wastes everywhere, create acid rain, deplete the rain forests, and tolerate wars, holocausts, ethnic cleansing, shifts in the weather, prejudice and hate, insane health care, an out-of-balance judicial system, an educational system that is failing us all, and a despicably inane political system.

In the insane asylum, your days might look like this:

You go to work at the crack of dawn, come home late, have a couple of beers or a piece of cheesecake (my personal choice), watch the "news" on TV, go to sleep, wake up the next day and do it all over again. And in this day and age, you probably head out at 6 am and get home at 9 pm—and work at a job you probably don't like! You may be in a relationship that's not working. And you sit in your little mud puddle of discomfort saying things like "TGIF" and "I hate Mondays," and your mud puddle seems like comfort because you've been there for so long. You don't know there is a way out, and if you could see it, your fear of change would probably stop you—or you wouldn't believe it could actually be created—especially by you.

You take your two weeks off in the summer (if you're lucky!) and basically live by the belief that life's a bitch, you pay taxes (another lie), and then you die.

Now if you're conscious enough to have picked up this book, all this probably sounds either incredibly sad or totally untrue. However, if you look around this world of ours, you'll quickly see that all of these things I describe are actually going on out there.

Now please don't get me wrong. I'm not a complete cynic nor do I think I walk on water. I'm just like everyone else (because, after all, we really are oneness!), moving toward greater consciousness as I'm practicing and allowing my true knowing to guide me. And I realize that here on Planet Earth things will probably never be perfect, at least not this trip around, because this is a place where we're all choosing how to be.

The behavior that I described is simply *unconsciousness* and it's nothing new. It goes back trillions of years—we've long been conditioned and programmed to be this way. Since the world never gave out guidebooks about how to create our reality (though they are available now!), most of us have simply been waiting to see what life would serve up to us.

Our existence on Planet Earth has been a trial and error process (with emphasis on "error"). In other words, we simply kicked back and accepted the lies, points of views, beliefs (energy) others had already established — and by doing so fell into the mass programming, which is unconsciousness.

(Remember, it's much easier to control those who live in unconsciousness vs. those who live in freedom and possibility, which is a great way to describe consciousness.)

In order to leave the insane asylum, we need to be able to look at that unconsciousness, be aware of it and then go into our own knowing, no matter how uncomfortable it might be and no matter what the fuck it takes. By the way, as I tell all my clients and students all the time, if you don't have some discomfort in your life, you are moving too slow!

Believe me, I get that it's much more comfortable to run and hide under the bed than to acknowledge what your life could be — what magic and potency might be possible for you. However, if you have gotten this far in this book, you are one of those in the minority who are conscious and want to be even more so — and I applaud you!

I invite you to step out of the insane asylum and into the vast landscape that awaits you. Out here you may just catch a glimpse of new possibilities for your life, possibilities that allow for miracles, magic and joy.

Hey, if *So Delicious* can come up with Cashew Caramel Crunch non-dairy ice cream that tastes as good as Ben and Jerry's, anything is possible!

**If I were truly creating my life today what
one thing can I choose right away?**

Everything that is, I now destroy and uncreate. POD POC.

Here are a few more questions for you:

**What would MY life be like if I showed up as if
anything was possible?**

What if I actually believed that whatever I set out to do and BE I would accomplish?

Who could I be if I was actually choosing FOR me?

WOW! Get the energy of that!

Okay, so you've gotten through the first three action steps and it's all feeling pretty light and exciting. Now you're ready for the really good stuff that will totally change your life. Right?

Wrong!

Nothing out there is going to change your life. You are going to change your life, *only you!* And this moment is your point of power — the moment when you will take action and choose for YOU. Remember, tomorrow never comes; it is always out there somewhere, just hanging around. If you want to know what you'll be like 10 or 20 years from now, the answer is pretty simple: You will be exactly as you are today, only older, unless you choose to change now.

This change takes work. I won't lie to you. It takes leaving your safe little mud puddle and venturing out on the most important exciting and scary adventure of your life. (Remember, it requires doing whatever the fuck it takes — and that's not for the faint of heart!) On this journey, there will be times when you want to run and hide, or when you will break up in hysterical laughter or weep tears of relief. And, really, isn't that what being here on Earth is all about?

With Access, however, you now have the greatest energetic tools and the language of consciousness so you can change and expand your possibilities with more ease.

No one ever taught you there was another way — a way to open up to the magnificence of the world and who you really BE. You probably didn't learn when you were a child that you are an infinite being having a physical experience to see what you can create and choose. You probably didn't learn that you are here to let go of your past; release your decisions, judgments, conclusions, projections, expectations, separations; and know who you really are. Right?

You didn't learn it as a child, but I'm here to tell you now. You are here to discover the magic and miracles that only you can create. You are a magician and a creator. All you need is to choose the willingness to be who you truly are, and see that there is another world right outside the walls of the insane asylum.

Moving out of the insane asylum means choosing a path of change…it means becoming conscious. YOU, the infinite being, have guided you right here. You can't find me or Access unless you're choosing consciousness and choosing for YOU.

As I have said, you have to be willing to do "whatever the fuck it takes!" All the fears of not fitting in, not having friends, being disowned by your family, or your husband leaving, or you wanting to leave and staying — all of these are reasons and justifications for why people don't choose consciousness, for why people stay in the insane asylum.

The bottom line is that you have to be willing to say that no matter what changes, no matter what shifts, no matter what you gain or leave behind, you say, *"I am going for this. I'm doing this. I'm being this. I'm having this. I'm choosing this…not matter what that fuck it takes!!"*

What have I made so vital, valuable and real about marginally committing to my life that keeps me in the starts and stops and the eradication of total possibility as often as I think?

Everything that is, I now destroy and uncreate. POD POC.

ACTION TOOL:
500,000 Miles

Close your eyes and be aware of your energy — your aware-ness — and expand out. Don't stress about perfection; this will just occur because you're asking for it. Fill your body, like it's a baby beach ball you're going to blow up in all directions. Expand the energy to fill your body. Fill your house. Keep expanding out, 360 degrees in all directions so that you're filling your whole city, your whole state, and the whole country — moving out around the world, then out to 200,000 miles, 300,000 miles. 500,000 miles. You will prob-ably start feeling light because you're being more of the infi-nite being you are.

Now that you are out here, Welcome Home! This is probably the closest you've been to the real YOU. Then ask yourself: If I were the infinite being that I truly be — who would I be right now? Just experience that energy/awareness because it's going to be very different than your normal space. The more you do his, the more expansive it will be. It's like going to the gym. Doing your sit-ups a few days in a row doesn't show a change, however, after a while, it will. Do this a few times a day, and watch your awareness change.

If you'd like a recording of this tool, you can find it at www.barbragilman.com

How to Stay Outside the Insane Asylum

When you feel yourself being pulled back into the insane asy-lum — as you probably will — a few things might be happening. You may be allowing your past to keep sneaking in and pulling you back so that you are right back in your "stuff" — the lie and the trauma and drama. Or you're projecting yourself so far ahead that you actually feel the potency of what could be and that freaks you out because it's so big.

What have I made so vital, valuable and real about creating the resistance of possibility that keeps me living as though everything is impossible and the only thing that is really possible is the limitations, rightness and judgments of this reality?

Everything that is, I now destroy and uncreate. POD POC.

Yes, this pull back to the insane asylum is part of the journey. It happens to me. Wouldn't it be cool to have magical tools and a language to give you awareness of the trauma and drama so you don't have to stay there?

Well, here are the tools and this is the language.

For me, the key is to remember who I am BEING. That is my bottom line. When I show up not choosing the power and potency, who am I being? Am I truly being me? I'm being some past me or I'm being a me who has given up my power and potency because the past is trying to creep in.

Joseph Campbell said, "Where you stumble, there your treasure is!" And he was right. Don't worry about being wrong, step outside the insane asylum and your gift will be revealed to you. That is the biggest gift on the planet. And that gift is YOU.

We each have access to the one thing that could truly change things — and we treat it like an item on our to-do list. It's yet another thing you have to do. It's like the old story of the woman who prays at church every Sunday and then goes home to attack her husband with the vacuum cleaner. It's very easy to declare yourself a conscious person; it's quite another thing to live as one.

There are more and more people around the world who are opening their eyes from that deadly sleep of unconsciousness and recognizing they've been living in the insane asylum. **Consciousness is the only way we're going to create the change that allows our planet to thrive.** What a miracle—our species is finally evolving. (Won't it be great to walk on two legs at last?)

In a time of transition, such as the one our planet is going through now, choosing for you through consciousness will create your greatest possibility for a life and living that actually works.

Asking for Advice from the Inmates

One of our big problems is that we keep listening to the insanity from inside the insane asylum—because we believe we're wrong and stupid and that everyone else knows more than we do because they have the money or the initials after their name.

Let me ask you a question. Say your friend had a cousin in the insane asylum. Your friend asked you to come visit with her. Would you go up to one of the inmates and ask for financial or relationship advice? It might sound crazy, however, we all do that. All the time!

It's no different than you going to the person who has written a book or earned 6 figures and asking their advice. To do that you give up your own knowing—you conclude that because this person has what you *think* you want, they can give you an answer. Here's the thing: That's their life that they created using their own **GPS.** It's not yours. You have your own GPS, which you access by asking questions and receiving your own awareness.

So, where in your life do you go into the insane asylum and ask the inmates for help?

The antidote is NOT to go back into the insane asylum and instead to start making choices by your own knowing. To be willing to know that you know.

Everywhere I'm pretending not to know what I really know, I now destroy and uncreate. POD POC.

The Lie of Prayer

People who pray to God don't understand that God doesn't speak in words. When a woman prays something like: "God, I don't have money! I'm so desperate!" God receives that energy of fear, lack and desperation. God (or the Universe) then says, "OK, Millie Smith in Chicago is asking for more lack, fear and desperation! Let's send her more of that!"

It might sound ridiculous, however, remember that the Universe has no judgment—it's simply consciousness. There is no right or wrong. So when Millie inadvertently asks for more lack—to the universe it's not right or wrong, it's just an energy! "That's cool," the Universe says, "Millie wants more fear and lack—let's send her more of that energy."

Instead, Millie could hold the energy of "I have so much money—it's flowing into my life." And she could ask questions like, "What would it take for me to have more money than I could ever imagine with ease?"

For you, when an unexpected bill comes, instead of going into the fear, ask a question: "What energy can I be to create all the money that is required for this bill?"

The old idea that more pain, harder work, and paying your dues are what leads to success is just part of the lie. Who do you think made that one up? The guy at the top of the pyramid or the one at the bottom of the food chain? Duh!

If you play more and go on vacation more, you'll see you're creating more money because you're in the energy of play - you're out beyond the limitation, you're not in the fear asking questions like: "How the hell am I going to pay for this?"

You're probably asking things like, "How do I create even more of this play and fun in my life?" or "What would it take for me to be the energy of money so that it will come and play with me?" Now, that changes things!

Money Game to Play with a Friend

Pretend you and I are friends and we both want to have more money. Instead of complaining and kvetching about money when we talk, we'll agree to get on the phone and I'll say, "I can't believe how much money I have in my life right now!" and you'll say something like, "I know, Barbra, I have three vacations coming up!"

Then I'll say, "Right! I'm so excited to take the next Access class and I can't wait to go shopping tonight for the fabulous shoes I've been dreaming of."

Here are some great questions to ask every day to get out of the insane asylum. (I've included lots more questions at the end of the book.)

What am I pretending not to know that I really know?

What awareness can I be to change everything that's not working for me?

What grand and glorious adventure will I have today?

What would it take for me to be a greater contribution to consciousness?

What can I create today that is even greater than yesterday?

What's possible that I haven't even acknowledged?

Chapter 5

ENTER CHAOS

Chaos. We avoid it. We dread it. We fear it. Why?

Because we've misidentified and misapplied what it is. When you get the true width and breadth of it, you see that chaos is the energy of total creation. For so long, we've been living in the energy of total *structure (which we also call "order")* — the opposite of chaos — and it has kept us imprisoned in the insane asylum.

Everywhere I've misidentified and misapplied chaos as turmoil, I now destroy and uncreate. POD POC.

Choosing chaos over order would open us up to everything that could be possible that we've never considered or acknowledged as possible. I know this a big concept to understand, so I've saved it for the last chapter.

We are energy. OK, I know you've heard that a lot, however, do you really *own* it? Are you living it? We are energy. The energy present in the mitochondrial cells of one single human could run the city of San Francisco for three months. I can hear your "WOW!" from my living room in Oregon. Yes, you are that powerful.

Now, in mid-2017 as I'm writing this book, the chaos energy around us is hard to miss.

Just look at politics as a fantastic example of what I mean by chaos. Politics was always a *structure*. Whatever your party was, you stuck with that. If your parents were Republicans, chances are you would be, too. Voting was your patriotic duty. Now in this new place we're in, it has to show up this way—party loyalty is gone, people consider not voting as a way to protest, Republicans and Democrats are both scratching their heads. This 180-degree change showed up with and through this chaos energy, knocking us right out of the structure of the past.

In the last presidential election, people said things like, "Who you going to vote for, the devil or Hitler?"

And many said, "Well, I'm just not going to vote." *This*, my friend, is chaos energy at work at an alpha level.

Why is Chaos Good?

Well, first let's talk about why we want so badly to have order. We want to have it so we can have control and everything will turn out the way we want it to.

That's how we look at it. However, that would be us looking for a *result*. When you're looking for a result (which is always something from the past) nothing greater than the result you've imagined can show up. This pretty well keeps you in your past. (It's very much like the Princess fantasy dreams I was talking about earlier.)

In the insane asylum, chaos is not considered a good thing. Not at all. If you're a person who moves quickly from activity to activity, people ask, "Why are you so chaotic?" "Why do you change your mind so much?" "Why don't you just settle down and stick to one job, career, marriage, home....?"

We are so entrained to the wrongness of chaos as if it is turmoil. It's one of the things we're taught to stay away from. We believe that without structure, without order, our life is not going to work. However, if we continue to choose order, we never get to see what's possible when we're being chaos — the amazing potent magical creator we truly be.

Everywhere that I've been trying to impel order into my life so I can finally be right, rather than functioning from the gift of chaos, I now destroy and uncreate it. POD POC.

Now, here's where it gets interesting. I'm not saying being chaos energy is being like PigPen in the Peanuts cartoons with dust and dirt swirling all around you. (This is what my clients always imagine.) There are places for order. You want to have a pinch of it in your life. It's like a creating a new recipe — like adding a bit hot jalapeno to a sweet and familiar cookie recipe. Isn't creation energy (chaos) wild and amazing? It is a wild energy — it's so big and limitless.

We want to create with is that little bit of order. Organization works with the chaos. It is not ORDER. It's a system, like a filing system. Organization assists you in working with the chaos. It's tremendous creation energy. You have so many ideas! Let me get organized…I'll make a folder for all my wild book ideas. That is very good. Organization is a wonderful tool to use with the chaos energy. You want to be organized. That will help you enter chaos with JOY, EASE and PLAY.

Because it's so big and wide, you can use your tool of organization so you don't get lost in chaos. For instance, I adore organization in my house — visually, that's the designer in me. I like to have things where I can find them.

When making choices, though, I ask questions to invite in the chaos:

What gifts am I not acknowledging here?

What possibility do I have here that I'm not aware of?

What am I not aware of that if I would be aware of it would change everything?

What contribution am I refusing to be that if I would be it would change the world?

That will give you the awareness of: "Why the fuck is this going on?" If I weren't in this energy then this and this and this wouldn't have occurred. In the moment, we don't know what's going on. Most people get into overwhelm or fear or judgment (as I've described in earlier chapters) and can't get the awareness because they are looking for a specific result, which has limited the possibility of something greater showing up.

Look at peoples' lives — we try to have control over everything. Everything. Money, family, emotions, food. We were ordered into this state — and if we don't have control, we jump into the fear. We measure, chart, plan, expect. A control freak is a control freak because they were ordered into the yearning for control.

We have been taught to believe that chaos is destructive. Actually, order is a *contraction* of what is possible. Chaos is undefinable; it is peace and consciousness. It's where everything you desire exists. When you are willing to be present with chaos, everything changes and you can be in total allowance and peace, creating something greater.

However, in this reality, consciousness is not order. Consciousness is chaos and chaos is necessary for creation.

Most of us get incredibly uncomfortable when we're "out of order." You want to have the cohesiveness and the communion between the order and chaos. Let me put it as simply as I can — I want you to get this: Keep your affairs organized, and always allow for more to be possible than the limited results you have in mind. That is what makes everything work. Use organization as the sidekick of chaos. Use it like you're tying up a package with a ribbon.

We live in polarity making everything good/bad, right/wrong or positive/negative. Chaos is not all good and order is not all bad. And vice versa. Again, you want that communion between them.

Look at it this way: Maybe the recipe didn't call for it, however the last little drop of cayenne pepper you decided to add to the batter is what made that cake so amazing. A lot of chaos…a bit of order….See what I mean?

What can we create together to create an amazing communion beyond this reality?

Most people think that if I do everything this way, and keep order in what I do and say, then life is going to turn out the right way, the way I have been told it would. After all, I'm being a perfect, right and good person, aren't I? Don't good things come to good people?

The truth is that chaos is the contribution that creates our lives and allows the planet to work.

What have I made so vital valuable and real about the order of always living as less that keeps me from the chaos of always establishing and actualizing me as more?

Everything that is, I now destroy and uncreate. POD POC.

Why We Get So Attached to Order

A child is born. Then she is told that she is wrong and why she is wrong. That becomes the lie she cannot go beyond. She's told, "You're wrong. Don't be so loud. Don't use that tone. Don't wear your hair like that." The parent considers their job to "order" the child and believes they have to be a good parent who has a good child who fits in so everyone else will acknowledge that they are a "good parent." We call this Point of Order, or POO. (And you know what poo is!)

I love looking at words and how we use them.

In order to attempt to create order, we give orders.

Such as: "You're in the Army now and these are your orders."

How we are supposed to look. How much we should weigh. How our hair, eyes, skin should appear. What we should drive, eat, wear, watch on Netflix, how much we sleep, how much we complain about our job. Everything is ordered—because they (our parents and our world) are impelling those orders. We then take over their job and impel those orders on ourselves.

Back to the algorithms. Everything, EVERYTHING around us is giving us orders to show up small and pathetic. To never be the inconceivable, infinite beings we truly BE. The structure of this planet is never to let you totally know that you are a potent, powerful, amazing creator and magician. If you knew you couldn't be controlled—well, game over!

Our government says it wants us to be the greatest, USA #1, the land of plenty. That is a lie. We have been ordered to show up as small, pathetic, stressed out, and disappointed. We take that on and then we, in turn, give that order to our being and our body. How much sleep we need, how fat we are, the fact that we are stuck in the "middle class," and so on.

When you're a little child and your mother tells you to drink your milk because it builds your bones, you take that order and impell it in your body. That is how your body then functions because you gave it the order. You need the milk because if you don't have enough, your bones will get brittle and your teeth will get cavities. Your body starts to need the milk. The same goes for the order we receive that if you eat a lot of sugar, you will have ADD or gain weight, etc. You eat sugar and you get all antsy or you get fat.

What have I made so vital valuable and real about the Point of Order (POO) of my past, that keeps me from creating a life that actually works for me?

Everything that is, I now destroy and uncreate. POD POC.

Look at relationships. We have been ordered to look at every-thing in a certain way. For instance, someone puts their disgrun-tled point of view on you because they're not getting what they need and they believe you're the one who should provide it. The way to get around this "order" is not to try and bring balance, or logic, or more love to the relationship. The way to get around it is to bring chaos in with total allowance, creation and no judg-ment.

Everything in your life that's not working is there because you're trying to institute order in that area.

Look at the places in your life where things aren't working — and then look at where you are trying to institute order. For exam-ple, maybe you went broke after you started a budget. Or you gained weight when you began that new diet. You decided to go to therapy for your marriage and all hell broke loose. A way to change those outcomes would be to ask questions to receive the awareness to create the possibility of something different show-ing up.

Here's a question for the brave:

How much chaos can I instill in my marriage to change it?

Because we want to be perfect little girls and boys, we listen to our parents and our society. We perpetrate those lies in our bod-ies and in our lives.

When you get down to it (which I love to do), the ultimate or-der is death. Eventually, there is so much order in the body that it starts to die because we're turning off the potency, joy and magic. Does that blow your mind a little?

Look at the spiritual world. People say you have to be ground-ed and balanced. All of that is order. When they say you're not grounded, what they are actually doing is trying to limit you

ACTION TOOL:
Change Your Perspective

When something happens that you're not so excited about or that you're judging as wrong, here are the questions to ask:

What's the value of this experience?

What greatness do I have now that I wouldn't have had othewise?

What different point of view do I have about _____that I wouldn't have had?

What did I gain from this?

How much chaos can I add here to change this?

What can I now be or do differently that would create an even greater possibility?

Asking these allows you to realize that you chose this (whatever it is!) in order to change the world.

because you're showing up too chaotic and different for them. You could actually change that if you were being and playing with chaos.

When children play and laugh and BE chaotic, they are told to be quiet. We don't want them to be joyful and free. We want them to fit in with our order. Where did we get that from again? Oh, yes, our parents!

The lie is perpetrated from one generation to the next, making sure we never get to be the chaos and the potent powerful beings we are here to be. When we're toiling away like worker bees and slaves, doing a job that once belonged to three people, we're told we're irresponsible or could lose our job if we try to leave at 5 p.m. instead of staying late into the evening.

I had a client years ago who worked at the World Trade Center in a very high-powered job. Her wedding was coming up; she had her dress and had already sent out the invitations. One day, her CEO came to her and said, "I need you to go to San Francisco on June 10th."

She said, "But that's my wedding day!"

"There are 10 people younger than you waiting for your job," he replied.

She chose to change her wedding date.

Look at all the situations where you are like the powerful lion and the boss, parent, government, teacher, etc. is like the animal trainer with the whip, saying, "I order you to get back into your cage! Don't show up with joy and possibility because I can't control you!"

Here's the bottom line: You have to be willing to be the energy of chaos if you're choosing for you. That is not about being in order, which is about being perfect, right, and good while giving you up. It is about taking you back and out of the order. Right now, we are a controllable commodity. We listen to everyone else—remember, that's like going into the insane asylum and asking advice from the inmates.

The best way to thrive with chaos? Ask questions. Ask questions. Ask questions.

What's right about this I'm not getting?

What would it take for me to create every change that hasn't been available, by being the chaos I truly BE and have been hiding for all eternity?

What would it take for me to be willing to have more fun than I can imagine by being the chaos I truly BE?

How much chaos can I create in my money flows?

How much chaos can I add here to change this?

What would it take for me to institute chaos here?

How much chaos can I BE to awaken the magic on planet earth?

What would it take for me to be the chaos that would create a living that is always expanding, never contractive and always creating greater possibilities with every choice I make?

What have I made so vital, valuable and real about being controlled that keeps me from choosing and creating everything I would like to choose, create and be that will truly change my world!

And everything that is, I now destroy and uncreate. POD POC.

This type of order is perpetrated on us when we go into the insane asylum and ask the inmates for advice without asking ourselves questions and being in awareness. Think about the therapists, priests, doctors, financial advisors, coaches and friends you've gone to. All of them can be helpful; none of them are wrong. However, you tend to just take their advice rather than asking a question to see if that advice would work for you (e.g., "Would it be a contribution for me to work with this person or take this action?")

Most people go around in circles instead of going to another possibility. We've been brought up to think we need advice from someone "greater" than we are. We've bought the lie that we are wrong and can't trust ourselves because that lie was impelled upon us. We give up *everything* to this lie. We think we are pathetic because of the bank account, the body fat, the small house, etc. This is why we haven't created much change in the last several decades — we are going in circles and being kept in that lie. (Think of the Mobius strip.) We never get to the magic and creation energy that is right there for us.

If you've gotten this far in the book and resonate with this information, you're a **humanoid** (you might want to peek back at the Glossary) and there is a different possibility for you. The folks I mentioned above can be fantastic for humans because they live in order and it's ok for them — that's who they are. They do well with the status quo. (Humans aren't bad and humanoids aren't good — we need both!) Think about it: Humans go by what they've learned, what's happened to them, and what they've read. And for humans, that's perfect. It's not wrong at all. But for humanoids, that's like taking an ox cart from Oregon to New York City. Why would you want to work with old information if you have the opportunity to work directly with the universe?

You, the humanoid, are always looking for change. You always want to have more, better, greater — and why wouldn't you? It's a different system for us humanoids. You *have* to ask the questions for YOU and allow chaos, the creation force, into your life.

So what does willingness to allow the chaos look like?

Here's a story I love to tell. I once had a client who was diagnosed with cancer. Five years later, he told me this was the greatest thing that ever happened. At the point of diagnosis, he had a job that he hated, and he was totally depressed. It took getting cancer for him to leave his job. He now has a creative job he loves, he makes great money, he has time off to play and he loves his life. He didn't allow the chaos in the beginning — like everyone is upon such a diagnosis, he felt devastated and afraid — but he was willing to look at the possibility I presented to him. He began to ask the question: What's the value of having cancer and what if this is actually the change I was requiring? That was the magic. That willingness. He was making the choice.

When you say, "Show me what else is possible," the universe *will* show you what is possible. So invite the change. Invite the chaos. For my client, doing this got him off a path that sooner or later would have meant death because he was so miserable and angry. The value of it was to get him out of the misery. Now he says, "The cancer really was the energy of creation that came into my life."

If you can give up the resistance to what is going on around you, and if you can invite chaos, it creates the energy flow, and that is what opens new doors for you.

Resistance is the contraction of what is possible. What is possible is expansive—undefinable, uncontrollable, unstoppable. People are so afraid of it! However, consciousness and creation energy is where *everything* that we truly desire lives.

When you are truly functioning from consciousness, nothing can stop you.

The people who choose consciousness as a way of showing up in this world have lives that are *totally* different from these "ordered" lives I've described here. Everyone in our insane-asylum reality judges you based on your bank account, the neighborhood you live in or the car you drive. These things have nothing to do with joy or consciousness! You could have $10 in the bank and have a totally wonderful life. Although I have to say I choose to have it ALL—consciousness AND a full bank account. Why not? It's just a choice.

What have I made so vital, valuable and real about rejecting and refusing money that keeps me from the chaos that would create me having more than I can imagine?

Everything that is, I now destroy and uncreate. POD POC.

I recently was talking with a humanoid friend who is a talented teacher and healer. What she's doing right now is travelling the country. She does odd jobs on her travels. Someone will call her to cook for a party in one state, she'll do some massage and healing work, she'll dog-sit, she'll teach a workshop, and then she'll go to another place. And most people she encounters think she's crazy. They can only see that she's a professional with the potential for a good job and steady income and she's giving that up to do this healing work and travel. They judge her, saying, "What? You're on a permanent vacation?! Aren't you worried?"

Humans *always* judge creative and entrepreneurial humanoids. Humanoids by nature are willing to welcome chaos and live whatever the moment brings without any judgment. What they are doing changes on a dime because they're always asking questions to create the next greater possibility, unless they have bought the lie, lock stock and barrel!

Now, if you want to see beautiful chaos in action, go look at a pre-K or daycare. They are willing to play with chaos. Toddlers = chaos. They jump from toy to toy. They want to leave as soon as they arrive. They cry for applesauce, then take a single bite and suddenly yell for bread. They make you tear up the bedroom looking for the one teddy bear that's not there. They are willing to BE chaos.

They are more like animals. Animals willingly live and be chaos. You know how when there's a tsunami or wildfire, the wild animals survive? That's because they have a knowing and they follow it. They live in total awareness. They are tuned in. So they leave their home, their forest, their nests—they enter the chaos because they are aware and choosing for themselves. They act from their knowing; they are not trying to please others. They don't wait for the 6:00 news to tell them to leave.

Everything that doesn't allow me to be the knowing I truly could be, I now destroy and uncreate.

Because that's where order was impelled and robbed us of our knowing. We end up giving in and surrendering to everyone else and that takes away our freedom to create US. That same order takes away our knowingness or awareness and we take on other's energy as ours. We believe they know based on reasons and justifications like these: they are older, wiser, richer, thinner, wrote a book, or are speaking on a stage. Reasons and justifications are the lies we create against us.

What would it take for me to be the chaos master I truly BE?

Everything that is I now destroy and uncreate. POD POC.

An infinite being would never allow anyone to take away their freedom or their choice. We've been so entrained to the wrongness of change and of being inconceivable, that we keep giving ourselves up to the order that everyone else wants to keep us in so we can fit in their world without having to look at the possibility that there might be a different way that would actually work for us.

What's crazy is that we end up using the magic and creation energy against us. We buy into the order and we use the chaos against us.

Do you know how many people are calling me lately and saying, "OMG, Barbra, my life is so chaotic! I'm in such chaos. I have this monster in my life and I'm scared!" Even though they've been in my classes and learned what I've told you here, they are still so entrained to fear it and jump right back into defining the *turmoil* of their lives as chaos.

Now there are a lot of people who just won't understand what I'm saying.

They are entrained to believe that chaos is bad. However, there is that one percent who are truly willing to do whatever the fuck it takes to have them and a life that works and to be a contribution to the planet. Yes! I'm talking to you with a smile on my face, waving a banner to usher you on! Go, you!

Hello! Remember, chaos is creation and not turmoil. OK, so what would it take to start playing with it? ANYTHING is possible. Say that three times and click your heels!

How much chaos can I be that would allow me to be the magical, mystical and amazing being that I truly be for all of eternity?

Everything that is, I now destroy and uncreate. POD POC.

What is so cool is that the molecules of chaos are creation. They are moving around. They are creating right now. You can create by talking to the molecules and asking them to create the change that would work for you. Ask them questions like:

How much chaos can I instill here to change this?

Order is like flat-lining. When nothing is happening, nothing is happening! You might have money in the bank, a clean house, and kids doing what you tell them to do—however, you are not creating. You're stagnating. You're stuck.

When you feel that flat-lining, just ask:

How much chaos would it take to turn this around?

Chaos gives you every choice available in every moment. Order gives you one "right" choice—and that choice ties you back into the insane asylum. You wrack your brain and ask for advice from the inmates about how to make the right choice. Which way to go, which job, which guy, which investment, which neighborhood, which dress, which hairstyle, etc.

Be allowance. In allowance, things roll off your back like water off a duck.

Be willing to choose to be open to the chaos—with that little pinch of order just to make it work.

What Does It Look Like to Be Open to Chaos?

When something hasn't worked before, you think it won't ever work. That's a conclusion and a decision and they will both make you right—and unwilling to change or do something differently. To be open to chaos requires asking, "What am I unwilling to change that if I changed it would give me everything I've been asking for?"

A year ago I was getting my nails done. A couple came into the salon for pedicures. All of a sudden, the man slumped over, the side of his mouth drooping. He was having a stroke! Total turmoil ensued. The salon owner called 911, his wife panicked, customers stared, the nail technicians screamed and didn't know what to do. There was lots of noise and craziness and fear.

I had just come back from Costa Rica where I'd learned an amazing Access body process based on the chaos energy. I asked if this would be a contribution to the man. I got a YES and I went over in what felt like slow motion and put my hands on his body. I ran the process. I had no awareness of time. After maybe 15 minutes he came to, shook his head and opened his eyes. Everyone in the place was amazed! The EMTs arrived, ran a bunch of tests and said he was OK and that he didn't even need to go to the hospital. His wife thanked me again and again. I felt so grateful for having this body of work of Access Consciousness®.

In everyday life, we deny the magic that we are and that we can do to change everything. Because we have misidentified and misapplied chaos as turmoil, we never get to play with the magic. Magic is not even on the menu.

Think about it: The most incredible energy of creation on this planet, we call destructive and desperately try to keep it out of our lives. If that doesn't sum up the insanity, nothing does.

We never get to create with this energy, in fact, we do the opposite. Instead of getting their nails done that day, all those salon customers got a taste of what's possible beyond this reality.

Everywhere I'm resisting chaos and choosing order, so I never get to know, acknowledge and claim the gift of me, I now destroy and uncreate. POD POC.

We stagnate because we resist. We get stuck creating from others' energy. Like I've said, it's like going to your neighbors' house and pulling a pair of dirty underwear out of their hamper and wearing it. When I say this in a class, people always go, "Ewww!" In reality, we do this all the time.

Remember: In order to maintain the order, everyone orders everyone. (We call it Points of Order: POO!) You energetically mimic the order of the people around you beginning from childhood. Your parents and everyone around you have been ordered to live a good, fitting-in, and orderd life (which, by the way, is really just a nicer way of saying "a prison sentence"). You try to be the perfect, right and good child. When you're trying to be the good little girl or boy, you're giving YOU up for your parents' or others' point of view. You're mimicking them. You want to be and maintain the order of their world. However, by being that, you have to energetically become as small as the smallest element of order in their world.

All the POO (Points of Order) that define the parameters of me and my life, and keep me from creating something greater....

I now destroy and uncreate. POD POC.

It's limitation. Simply put, not a great choice!

Here's an example of how it works. You have a friend who doesn't like to go out in the rain. You want her to feel good and to love you. You want to allow her to have that order so she feels safe and comfortable. So, when you are together, even though you love going out in the rain and have so many things you want to do today, you stay in with her. You give you up and by doing that, you become the smallest element of what's possible for you.

You can't be bigger than her **order.** (And she's literally the one who's ordering you!)

And now you're fitting in and you don't ruffle her feathers. You are still part of her herd and you're validating her smallness. And in doing so, you give up the chaos and magic. You give up your possibility for being the amazing, incredible playful magician and creator you truly be.

What have I made so vital, valuable and real about the artificial reality of this world that requires me to lessen my magic in order to be here?

Everything that is, I now destroy and uncreate. POD POC.

What if that chaos of going out in the rain was an invitation to your friend to be more and greater? And what if you giving up you to validate her fear was not about loyalty or being a good friend, it was about limitation for both of you? You have the limitation of not doing what you love to do and she has the limitation of not stepping out of her comfort zone to change.

Chaos is the wind beneath your wings. It is honoring your awareness to expand all that you are.

You're in the mode of creation. You're flying through the sky with a magic wand! There is nothing you can't do or BE. Anything is possible! When you are in this mode you meet the people you need to meet. Ideas spontaneously come into your awareness. Resources become visible that weren't there the day before.

Magic!

That is what the chaos energy gives us.

Are you starting to see that it's not about fixing your problems? It's about so much more. It's about acknowledging that your life and the problems were a lie you were ordered into in the first place.

Access Consciousness® gives you a super-charged, totally different, energetic toolkit and the language of consciousness to create the possibility and contribution you and the planet require. To open the doors! To change your world and change the world!

That energy is what is REAL. And that energy is what will allow you to do whatever the fuck it takes to live the inconceivable, potent, amazing, magical life you are here to live!

Know that all the joy and ease and all the magic creation you hoped was real is real — and you can actually create it with chaos energy! The reason it doesn't seem possible is that you've been ordered to choose against you to fit in. You have tried to not have more or be more or better or greater than anyone else. You've tried to be a good girl, a good boy, a good friend, a good employee, daughter, brother, mother, wife, husband…

And look where that has gotten you.

So, would you give up the desire to fit in? Starting today, would you BE willing to be what is unimaginable to everyone around you?

Yes? Great! Let's go!

Now, you are ready to do and be whatever the fuck it takes!

What if you know that your problems aren't problems at all?

What if your problems are the possibilities that brought you to this book?

What if Access Consciousness® is the gift you've been seeking all along?

What if you passed this book along to someone else?

Here's a bit of home-play for you (because who wants to do home-work?)

Repeat these questions, followed by the clearing statement. I like to record them on my iPhone and play them back on a loop.

- What would it take for me to choose for me and be willing to be as inconceivable as I can be?

- What would it take for me to live with ease, joy and glory®?

- What would it take for me to be willing to be as inconceivable as I can be?

- What would it take for me to show up as the potent bitch when it's required, in total allowance?

- What would it take for me to use these tools every day so I can be the gift and invitation of ME?

- What would it take for me to keep playing, having fun, and creating with ease?

Remember...**it's about changing the fucking world by being you!**

And as I say goodbye, just one last reminder that the whipped cream on the dessert of life — the real purpose of being here on Planet Earth — is to have FUN and BE the delicious morsel of Joy, Magic and Creation. When you are BEing that contribution... that magical amazing incredible and potent you, YOU change the world!

Please KNOW that you're worth it. YOU are the gift the planet has been waiting for!

Thank you for coming on this journey with me. I'm choosing to know you've experienced the awareness that there is another possibility and you're excited to continue on this path and see what's possible—to see what's more, better and greater than what you've ever imagined before.

Now, if you're still asking, "What would it take for me to change my/the world?"

The answer is simple: You simply show up BEing YOU, whatever the fuck it takes!

What energy, space and consciousness can I be to generate, create and actualize a fantastic, amazing, unbelievable, phenomenal, magical and miraculous reality beyond this reality with total ease?

And for you who know you did come here to be one of those 100 monkeys—who know that you are here so the planet has a chance to not only survive, but to *thrive*—you will not let the draw of the ordinary pull you.

You will take this invitation.

You will keep showing up.

You will do whatever the fuck it takes!

Including passing this book on!

With love and gratitude,

Barbra

ACTION TOOL:
The Potency of Asking Questions

One of the greatest tools you have is to ask questions of the universe. The universe is a system of energy. We all know that prayer works—however, the one thing they kept from us is that God/Source/Higher Intelligence/Universe does not speak the language of words—it speaks the language of energy. It is like a candy machine. If you want a Snickers, you put in your money and enter, let's say, D-3. Your candy comes out.

The universe works the same way—except instead of coins, you put out your energy in the form of a question. The universe receives your energy and simply sends back to you the matching energy.

So, ask more questions!

Start a practice of asking questions all through the day. Asking questions reboots your being. It's different than you've been taught—and it works.

What else is possible?
What is right about me that I'm not getting?
What would it take for me to have ease and clarity?

MAGICAL BONUS QUESTIONS

What if my need to be understood is actually one of the greatest limitations to what I can BE and create in and as my life? **And everything that is, I now destroy and uncreate. POD POC.**

What have I made so vital, valuable and real about resisting my greatest capacity that keeps me stuck in living the limited life of this reality? **And everything that is, I now destroy and uncreate. POD POC.**

How much change am I now capable of choosing, that if I would choose it would change everything and create a life and living that totally works for me with total joy! **And everything that is, I now destroy and uncreate. POD POC.**

How much order am I using to create the absolutely totally irrevocable resistance and utter refusal of ease am I choosing? **And everything that is, I now destroy and uncreate. POD POC.**

What have I made so vital, valuable and real about the inevitability of limited possibility that keeps me creating as though I have no choice? **And everything that is, I now destroy and uncreate. POD POC.**

What have I made so vital valuable and real about results that keep me from creating beyond your limitations? **And everything that is, I now destroy and uncreate. POD POC.**

What's it going to take for me to not give me up for anyone and anything? **And everything that is, I now destroy and uncreate. POD POC.**

Would an infinite being choose this? **And everything that is, I now destroy and uncreate. POD POC.**

What would it take for me to be the energy that would create a conscious future? **And everything that is, I now destroy and uncreate. POD POC.**

YOUR DAILY PLAY SHEET

Every morning when you wake up:

- ✓ Expand your awareness 500,000 miles and lower all barriers.

- ✓ Ask: "Who am I today and what grand and glorious adventures will I be having today?"

- ✓ Say: Everything my relationship was with me yesterday, I now destroy and uncreate. POD POC. Use this process with everything and everyone in your life: your body, money, children, husband, dog, job, etc.

Through the day:

- ✓ What else is possible?

- ✓ How can it get any/even better than this?

- ✓ Universe, show me something beautiful!

- ✓ Can I have the money now, please?

- ✓ All of life comes to me with ease, joy and glory®.

- ✓ And always, "POD POC" anything that doesn't work for you!!

YOUR MAGICAL ACCESS CONSCIOUSNESS 6-STEP TOOLKIT

1. Choose.

Remember that CHOICE is the most potent tool you have available in every moment!

2. Use Your Personal GPS.

Does this have a sense of "heavy" or "light"?

Your truth will be light. That's a green light.

A lie (for you) will be heavy. Consider heaviness a red light

3. Clear.

When something has a sense of heavy and you don't want to hold onto it, say:

Everything this is, I now destroy and uncreate. POD POC.

Repeat until that sense is gone.

4. Return to Sender.

When you're sensing physical or emotional discomfort, ask:

"Who does this belong to?"®

If it goes away, then say, "Return to sender with consciousness."

If it doesn't go away, go back to # 3.

5. Interesting Point of View.

When you or someone else judges or says anything that has a sense of heaviness say: "Interesting point of view; I have this point of view." This creates a greater space of no judgment for you to function and create from!

6. Ask Daily Questions to the Universe:

What else is possible?

What's right about this I'm not getting?

What's right about me I'm not getting?

What's it going to take for me to choose for me?

What are the infinite possibilities in this moment?

What would it take for this to turn out better than I could've ever imagined?

How can it get any better than this?

What would it take to change this?

If I choose this, would it be expansive for me and everyone concerned?

What choice do I have?

What can I BE and do today to out create myself?

What am I aware of that I'm not acknowledging?

What question can I ask?

What contribution can I BE or receive?

What adventure can I have today that would make my life fun right away?

What gifts do I have than I'm not using?

How can I use this to my advantage?

What is this? What can I do with it? Can I change it?

How do I change it?

Will this work for me?

What do I have to do, be or change to make it work?

ACKNOWLEDGMENTS

This book was birthing itself in the most challenging and life-changing time of my life, and I knew it would require the assistance of a birthing coach. But who? Suddenly, she appeared — with the name Madeleine Eno — and showed up as the magical scribe who listened and wrote as I spoke at my classes, at my events, at my women's group, and over the phone. She effortlessly co-created with me and my authentic voice appeared on the pages with the clarity, energy, and intent with which it was given. What a gift to the world, and to me, that you are, Madeleine. Your essence is shared here with mine. Find Madeleine at www.inthewriteplace.com

To HF for designing the most wonderful book cover that matches the energy of the book so perfectly! You are Magic. YOU are LOVED!

WANT MORE?

For information about my life-changing classes, products and experiences in Access Consciousness®, visit www.barbragilman.com and be sure to download your free Access tool. (I love to travel, put a group together and I'll come to you!) You'll also find an audio recording of all the processes in this book!

Schedule a 1:1 session with me and watch how fast your life changes:
Email: barbra@barbragilman.com

Learn more about how I'm working with Access Consciousness and business at www.outoftheboxbusinesscoaching.com

Read more:
Dr. Dain Heer's book, *Being You, Changing the World,* is a must-read! Find it on Amazon or www.drdainheer.com

CPSIA information can be obtained
at www.ICGtesting.com
Printed in the USA
FFHW011230270119
50261014-55265FF